Swaziland

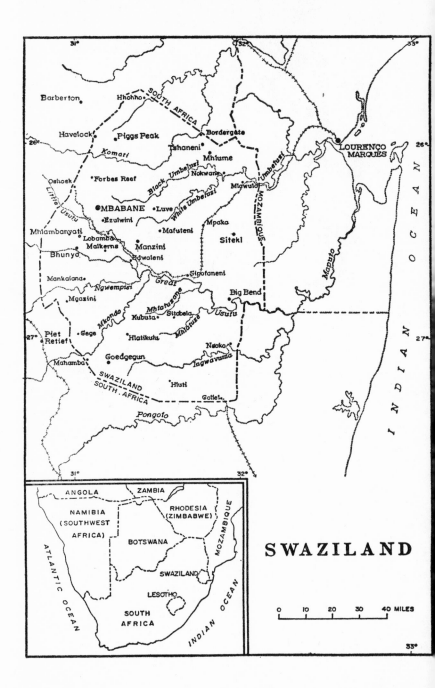

SWAZILAND

Swaziland

The Dynamics of
Political Modernization

Christian P. Potholm

UNIVERSITY OF CALIFORNIA PRESS

BERKELEY, LOS ANGELES, LONDON

To Erik, who was thought of

Contents

Preface

THIS STUDY AROSE OUT OF FIELD WORK CONDUCTED IN Southern Africa and Great Britain during the academic year 1965–1966, a trip made possible by a grant from the Shell Companies, Inc., awarded by the Fletcher School of Law and Diplomacy, and from follow-up work in Ghana during the summer of 1969, funded by Vassar College. The Faculty Research Committee of Bowdoin College also generously supported the preparation of this book.

The work owes a considerable debt to many persons. I should especially like to thank those Swazi and European officials, too numerous to mention, who so readily granted interviews; and I am extremely grateful for the helpful comments of Ben Cockram, Neville Rubin, Shelia Marks, John Spencer, Robert Stewart, Richard Stevens, Jordan Ngubane, and Carl Rosberg. In addition, His Excellency, Dr. S. T. Msindazwe Sukati, Ambassador of the Kingdom of Swaziland to the United States and High Commissioner in Canada, provided valuable assistance with the difficult and changing siSwati orthography. I am also most grateful for the editorial and secretarial assistance of Constance Parmalee, Donna Musgrove, Regina Paradis, and Gladys Peterson. Gig Babson, Philip Warwick, and Michael Hastings were of considerable help as research assistants, while William McClung and Diane Fairchild Beck at the University of California Press aided greatly in preparing the manuscript for publication. Finally, I owe a tremendous debt to my wife Sandra, who accompanied me in the field and who came to love the Swazis as much as I.

C.P.P.

Mbabane, Swaziland, 1965
St. Peter Mountain, St. Thomas, 1970
Brunswick, Maine, 1972

MEN FIGHT AND LOSE THE BATTLE AND THE THING THEY FOUGHT FOR COMES ABOUT IN SPITE OF THEIR DEFEAT, AND WHEN IT COMES, TURNS OUT NOT TO BE WHAT THEY MEANT AND OTHER MEN HAVE TO FIGHT FOR WHAT THEY MEANT UNDER ANOTHER NAME.

WILLIAM MORRIS
The Ballad of John Ball

I

The Ngwenyama and the Primacy of Tradition

THE PERIOD SINCE WORLD WAR II HAS WITNESSED A
marked decline in the political efficacy of many African traditional authorities, particularly those who have sought to play
a national political role. Many either could not compete effectively with their modern counterparts or were unable to maintain their previous privileged position. On balance, most lost,
rather than gained, political power with the independence of
their states. The mwami of Rwanda, the sardauna of Sokoto,
the mwami of Burundi, the kabaka of Buganda, the mora naba
of the Upper Volta, the litunga of Barotseland, and the king
of Lesotho, to name but the most prominent, have all had their
political roles circumscribed, reduced, or eliminated.

Seen in this perspective, the success of the ngwenyama of
Swaziland, Sobhuza II, offers a substantial amendment to the
widely held theory that modern political institutions, economic
development, and independence are necessarily inimical to traditional African authorities. It is true, of course, that there
have been other situations in Africa where traditional authorities have been able to cope with these new forces and to maintain their political positions.[1] But the magnitude of Sobhuza's

1. For a variety of examples, see Jean Suret-Canale, "The End of Chief-
taincy in Guinea," *Journal of African History* 7, no. 3 (1966): 459–493;
Peter C. Lloyd, "Traditional Rulers," in James S. Coleman and Carl G.
Rosberg, Jr. (eds.), *Political Parties and National Integration in Tropical
Africa* (Berkeley and Los Angeles: University of California Press, 1966),
pp. 382–412; Norman N. Miller, "The Political Survival of Traditional
Leadership," *Journal of Modern African Studies* 6, no. 2 (1968): 183–198;

triumph and the political expansion of the monarchy are un-
matched in recent African history. Sobhuza II began the 1950s
recognized only as a paramount chief. He entered the 1970s
not only as the king of the Swazis but as the king of all Swaziland, including its white, Eurafrican, and non-Swazi African
populations. With the attainment of independence on September 6, 1968, Sobhuza became the head of state with virtually
unchallenged political authority. All Swazi national land and
mineral wealth are vested in his office. His political party, the
Imbokodvo National Movement, holds all but three elected
seats in the national House of Assembly, while his personal
appointees occupy each nominated position in both the House
of Assembly and the Senate. His hand-picked choice, Prince
Makhosini, is the prime minister.

The ngwenyama's triumph is all the more remarkable when
one considers the constellation of forces arranged against him
and his allies within the traditional tribal hierarchy. On the
one hand, there were a number of British colonial officials, led
by Resident Commissioner Brian (later Sir Brian) Marwick,
who felt that the future of Swaziland lay with a one-man, one-
vote political arrangement dominated by detribalized political
leaders who would form modern political parties and who
would allow the ngwenyama to reign but not to rule. Secondly,
there were European settlers in Swaziland who attempted to
use the prestige and power of the monarchy to maintain their
own privileged economic and political position, as well as some
South African officials who saw in the political situation of
Swaziland an opportunity to legitimize the development of
Bantustans within South Africa through the formation of a
nearby, de facto Swazi homeland under a docile, friendly nominally independent king. Finally, there were the "modern" po-

Elliott P. Skinner, "The 'Paradox' of Rural Leadership: A Comment,"
Journal of Modern African Studies 6, no. 2 (1968): 198–201; C. S. Whitaker,
"A Dysrhythmic Process of Political Change," *World Politics* 19, no. 2
(1967): 190–217; and idem, *The Politics of Tradition: Continuity and
Change in Northern Nigeria* (Princeton: Princeton University Press, 1970).
An earlier analysis now somewhat overridden by events is found in two
works by David E. Apter, "The Role of Traditionalism in the Political
Modernization of Ghana and Uganda," *World Politics* 13, no. 4 (1960):
45–68; and *The Political Kingdom in Uganda*, rev. ed. (Princeton:
Princeton University Press, 1967).

litical figures themselves, primarily Swazis but also some Zulus, who espoused a variety of Pan-African concepts and who, initially at least, were dedicated to the destruction of the monarchy as a meaningful political force. In addition, subsuming this multidimensional struggle were a series of demographic and economic changes that further complicated the efforts of the ngwenyama to keep the Swazi cultural nation intact and to prevent a marked reduction in the monarchy's national political power.[2]

Faced with these challenges, Sobhuza II could have retired from the day-to-day political affairs of the country and allowed himself to stand as a revered, if somewhat impotent, figurehead. Instead, he chose to compete with his adversaries on their own terms and thrust himself and the monarchy directly into the political fray, risking both defeat and disgrace. As matters turned out—and not without substantial dramatic irony—the Swazi traditionalists proved to be very effective in the use of "modern" political techniques and actually used the intrusion of modernity to maintain and even expand their political power. In the case of Swaziland, there were a number of supportive factors that aided the traditional authorities in their quest for political hegemony. In subsequent chapters, we shall examine two of these in detail, the political expertise of Sobhuza II and the resiliency of the traditional political system. At this juncture, I wish to concentrate on another set of givens: the location of the political arena of Swaziland, the ethnic composition of that arena, the peculiar history of the Swazi people, and the components of the traditional Swazi political system that proved to be so adaptive in the 1960s.

Present-day Swaziland is a small country. Situated between Mozambique and the South African provinces of Natal and the Transvaal, it encompasses an area of 6,705 square miles. Ninety miles in width from east to west and a hundred and twenty miles in length from north to south, it lies between the 26th and 27th latitudes south and the 31st and 32nd meridians east. Despite its diminutive size, however, Swaziland has four distinctly different topographical and climatological zones,

2. The cumulative impact of these changes is covered in chapter 2 of this work.

which run from north to south and exist in parallel belts along its entire length.

The westernmost belt, lying astride the border between Swaziland and the Transvaal, is the high veld, known to the Swazis as *inkhangala*. The mountain ranges that make up the high veld average between 3,500 and 4,500 feet in altitude and contain two peaks, Bulembu and Ngwenya, of over 6,000 feet. The high elevation maintains a cool, almost temperate climate, with between 60 and 100 inches of rain annually. The administrative capital of Swaziland, Mbabane, is located in this belt, as are the large forestry projects at Bhunya and Piggs Peak and the Havelock asbestos mine complex.

Running parallel to the high veld to the east is the middle veld, referred to by the Swazis as the *umphakatsi,* or "headquarters" area, and regarded as the spiritual homeland of the nation. The elevation falls away rapidly from the high veld, averaging between 2,000 and 2,500 feet, although there are a number of hills whose heights exceed these levels. The middle veld is drier and hotter, with a subtropical climate. The commercial center of Manzini and the principal Swazi capital of Lobamba, as well as the new Parliament building, are found here. Within the middle veld are the major citrus projects of the Malkerns Valley, the industrial complex at Matsapa, and many cotton and tobacco farms.

Some twenty miles in width, the middle veld soon merges into the low veld. Called *ihlanze* by the Swazis, it is the driest and hottest area of Swaziland and has an average elevation of just over 500 feet. Semiarid, its flat, rolling plains are covered with thornbush and scrub vegetation. Since World War II, irrigation has transformed portions of the low veld into some of Swaziland's most productive agricultural areas with extensive cultivation of rice and sugar in the Tshaneni-Mhlume and Big Bend areas. Unlike many other countries in Southern Africa, Swaziland is well watered with major rivers—such as the Komati, Lomati (Mlumati), Great and Little Usutu (Lusutfu) —originating in the high veld and flowing eastward into Mozambique and the Indian Ocean. Running the length of the low veld and separating Swaziland from Mozambique is the impressive escarpment of Lubombo. This nearly flat plateau rises like a wall out of the low veld and is broken only occasionally by a number of gorges through which the rivers of Swaziland flow to the Indian Ocean. Its climate and elevation approximate those of the middle veld and it is used primarily for ranching and subsistence farming. Siteki is the only town of any size.

Of greater political consequence than the size and topography of Swaziland is its location and the ethnic composition of its population, for Swaziland's size (6,705 square miles) and population (381,000) are dwarfed by its neighbors. South Africa and Mozambique have 18 and 7 million persons, respectively, and 500,000 and 300,000 square miles, while Rhodesia has a population of 4.5 million persons and an area of 150,000 square miles. Even the other two former High Commission Territories with which it is so often compared, Lesotho and Botswana, are far larger and more populous.[3] Lesotho has nearly three times the population and twice the area, while Botswana has nearly twice the population and over thirty times the area.

Also of consequence is the fact that during decolonization the surrounding areas were controlled by white minority governments or colonial authorities who provided an enclosed, insulated environment for Swaziland during most of the 1950s and 1960s. The circle of white-dominated states kept Swaziland out of the full force of the winds of change for over a decade so that, even when political and ideological intrusions occurred, their impact was muted. In this tiny enclave in Southern Africa surrounded by European-run governments, the Swazi traditional authorities could contest their modern African rivals far more easily than if they had been struggling in a more open, less controlled context. If the contiguous countries had been run by Africans who favored the "modern" political elements, for example, events might have turned out differently. As it was, the ngwenyama and his followers were

3. Many existing works on the former High Commission Territories of Swaziland, Basutoland (now Lesotho), and Bechuanaland (now Botswana) have emphasized the connections among them. While it is true that all three were considered as a group by the British colonial authorities, there is currently very little political, economic, and social interaction among them.

supported not only by the European presence but by the conflicting views of two European groups, the South African government and the British colonial authorities. The Swazi traditionalists had the opportunity to play one off against the other
and to use the very context of Southern Africa to their advantage. We shall return to these important factors in the following chapters.

If the Swazi traditionalists were aided by the international
environmental context which reduced the force of the exogenous inputs and afforded them room for political maneuver,
they were also assisted by the demographic homogeneity of
Swaziland. Unlike most other African countries, where the traditional political elites had to contend not only with modern
political elements within their own ethnic units but also with
other ethnic units, the Swazi authorities were aided by the
fact that their political area more or less coincided with their
ethnic group. As of 1966, the population of Swaziland was
381,000, of whom 9,000 were Europeans, 4,000 were Eurafricans, and just over 20,000 were non-Swazi Africans, primarily
Zulu and Shangana.[4] The rest of the population was Swazi.
In essence, Sobhuza II had an existing cultural and linguistic
nation which for all intents and purposes prevented the colonial authorities and the white settlers from playing off one
ethnic group against another and which hindered the growth
of modern parties, since fully 87 percent of the Swazis were
living in the countryside as subsistence farmers and 97 percent
were illiterate. As of 1966, there were over 350,000 affiliates of
the Swazi nation living outside the borders of Swaziland, primarily in South Africa; but the links between these Swazis
and the tribal core had been weakened during the past century, and during the period under review there was virtually
no sentiment in Swaziland for a "gathering in" of these
persons.

Much has been written about the dysfunctional aspects of
"tribalism," and certainly ethnic rivalries have been disrup-

4. H. M. Jones, *Report on the 1966 Swaziland Population Census*
(Mbabane: Government Printer, 1968); and P. Smit, "Swaziland: Resources and Development," *Swaziland on the Eve of Independence* (Pretoria: Africa Institute of South Africa, 1969), pp. 15–31.

tive, even corrosive, in their impact on political systems in Nigeria, Congo (Kinshasa), Kenya, Rwanda, and the Sudan.[5] Yet given other examples of peaceful interaction (as in Tanzania), it would seem that ethnicity per se is not destructive. Rather, it is the relationship between the ethnic group and the state, and the relationship among the various ethnic groups that make up the state, which determine the impact of ethnicity on the polity. If the ethnic group more or less coincides with the state, as do the Sotho in Lesotho and the Somalis in the Somali Republic, ethnicity becomes an important factor aiding in political integration by reducing centrifugal strains. This was certainly the case in Swaziland and was to have profound repercussions for the drive for political hegemony undertaken by the traditional authorities.

Of paramount importance in the political struggle that developed after 1950 was the cohesion of the Swazi cultural unit and the adaptability of the traditional political system. Before analyzing these ingredients in some detail, it is necessary to sketch briefly the history of the Swazi people.

Their early history is by no means clear. Swazi oral tradition claims the existence of a Swazi nation extending back into time through the rule of twenty-five kings, but the Swazis themselves can agree only on the last eight.[6] It seems likely that the Swazi, like other of the Nguni people, gradually pushed south from central Africa during the fifteenth and sixteenth centuries. Early in the sixteenth century, one group, the Dlamini clan, settled in the area of Delagoa Bay in what is now Mozambique. There, under the leadership of a chief-

---

5. Although in this regard, I would agree with Richard Sklar that "tribalism" has been overworked as an explanation of political phenomena in Africa. As he rightly points out, ethnicity is used to mask personal or class competition; see Richard L. Sklar, "Political Science and National Integration," *Journal of Modern African Studies* 5, no. 1 (1967): 1–11. Immanuel M. Wallerstein has also indicated the ways in which ethnicity may actually serve to increase national integration and political development; see "Ethnicity and National Integration in West Africa," *Cahiers d'Etudes Africaines* 3, no. 1 (October 1960): 129–139.

6. Hilda Kuper, *The Swazi: A South African Kingdom* (New York: Holt, Rinehart, and Winston, 1963), p. 7. For a fuller account of the early history of the Swazi people, see her *An African Aristocracy: Rank Among the Swazis* (London: Oxford University Press, 1947), pp. 1–18.

tain known as Ngwane II, they began to call themselves Bantfu Baka Ngwane, the people of Ngwane. This consolidation separated them from the main southward thrust of the Nguni migrations, and it was only after several generations on the coast that they moved west, across the Lubombo escarpment in the late eighteenth century into what is now southern Swaziland. There, two Swazi kings, Ndvungunye and Sobhuza I, attempted to consolidate their hold over this area, but their control was never secure due to the Zulu and Ndwandwe incursions from the south.[7]

Under mounting pressure, Sobhuza I led his people farther north into central Swaziland. This migration took place during 1820 and brought the group into contact with the Sotho inhabitants of the area. Militarily less advanced, these people were absorbed. The Swazis, however, avoided pitched battles with Zulu forces and only once, in 1838 after the Boer trekkers had defeated the Zulus under Dingane, did the Swazis fight and win a major battle with them. Sobhuza I died the next year and was succeeded by his son Mswati. Mswati was the greatest of the Swazi warrior-kings and left his name to his several thousand people and their language. He unified the various clans and instituted a number of military-political innovations borrowed from the Zulu: the age-regiment system that cut across clan lines, new military tactics, and new weapons technology.[8] Mswati was highly successful in amalgamating a tribal nation; and at the height of his career, his domain extended from the Pongola River in what is now South Africa to the southern reaches of Rhodesia.[9] In spite of the Swazi suc-

7. Leonard Thompson, 'The Zulu Kingdom," in Monica Wilson and Leonard Thompson (eds.), The Oxford History of South Africa (London: Oxford University Press, 1969), 1:336–364; and J. D. Omer-Cooper, The Zulu Aftermath (Evanston: Northwestern University Press, 1966).

8. For an account of the revolution in warfare initiated by the Zulu, the interested reader should consult the Thompson and Omer-Cooper works mentioned in n. 7, above, as well as Max Gluckman, "The Kingdom of the Zulu of South Africa," in M. Fortes and E. E. Evans-Pritchard (eds.), African Political Systems (London: Oxford University Press, 1940), pp. 25–55; A. T. Bryant, Olden Times in Zululand and Natal (London: Longmans, Green, 1929); and Donald R. Morris, The Washing of the Spears (New York: Simon and Schuster, 1965).

9. Kuper, An African Aristocracy, p. 16.

cesses against their northern and eastern neighbors, the Zulus continued to harry them; and after a particularly devastating Zulu raid in 1854, Mswati appealed to the British agent general in Natal, Sir Theophilus Shepstone, for protection. The British had only recently annexed Natal (1843) and were unwilling to take on the responsibility for protecting the Swazi, but Shepstone was able to use his influence to help curtail the Zulu attacks. From this point on, the Swazis often allied themselves with the Europeans, fighting, for example, with the British against the Bapedi and with the Boers against the Mabhoko.

During the reign of Mswati, the entire complexion of Southern Africa was altered as European expansion increased. The Orange Free State and the Transvaal Republic declared their independence in 1854 and 1860, respectively, and subsequent movement by the British inland from Natal and the Cape Colony set the stage for future conflict between the British and the Boers as well as for interaction between these groups and the various African polities.[10] During the reign of Sobhuza I, traders had visited the area; but until the middle of the nineteenth century, these contacts had been highly sporadic and transitory. Subsequently, however, Europeans began to settle permanently and to ask for a variety of concessions concerning land, mining opportunities, and commercial monopolies. To Mswati falls the dubious honor of being the first Swazi king to grant a recorded concession (in 1861). It was Mswati's good fortune to die before these concessions and their concomitant problems became widespread.

Upon the death of Mswati in 1868, an adolescent boy, Ludvonga, was chosen to be the next king, but he died mysteriously. After a period of bitter feuding, a group of princes agreed to support one Mbandzeni for the throne, but with

10. The convoluted story of these interactions is covered in Eric Walker, *A History of Southern Africa* (London: Longmans, Green, 1957), pp. 1–539; C. W. De Kiewiet, *A History of South Africa* (London: Oxford University Press, 1957), pp. 1–114; Wilson and Thompson, *The Oxford History of South Africa*, pp. 187–446; Eric Walker (ed.), *The Cambridge History of the British Empire*, 8 (Cambridge: Cambridge University Press, 1963); and Kuper, *An African Aristocracy*, pp. 19–33. For a more off-hand account, see Owen R. O'Neil, *Adventures in Swaziland* (London: Allen and Unwin, 1921).

Ludvonga's mother as the queen regent. Mbandzeni was apparently a peace-loving man in a violent era and readily acquiesced to European pressures for a variety of concessions. Mbandzeni continued his reckless grants until "Practically the whole area of the country was covered two, three or even four deep by concessions of all sizes, for different purposes and for greatly varying periods. In but a very few cases were even the boundaries defined; many of the areas had been subdivided and sold several times and seldom were the boundaries of the superimposed areas even coterminous." [11] In fact, by the conclusion of his reign, over half the land of Swaziland was in the hands of Europeans. The Swazis continue to maintain that these concessions were not granted in perpetuity. Although Mbandzeni received considerable amounts of money for the concessions, he was disturbed by what was happening to his country but apparently felt himself too weak to do much about it: "I know the concessions are bad, but I have white men all around me. By force they have taken the countries of all my neighbors. If I do not give them rights here they will take them. Therefore I give them and they pay. Why should we not eat before we die." [12]

Mbandzeni was not incorrect in assuming that more powerful forces were at work; soon after his statement, the British government and the South African Republic signed two conventions, one in 1881 and the other in 1884. Ostensibly designed to protect Swazi "independence," they actually allowed the South African Republic to incorporate vast portions of the territory claimed by the Swazi nation.[13] Further interest in Swaziland was spurred by the discovery of gold in 1882;

11. Lord Hailey, *Native Administration in the British African Territories* (London: His Majesty's Stationery Office, 1953), p. 363. See also his *African Survey* (London: Oxford University Press, 1957), pp. 497–517, where he refers to the situation in Swaziland as "parallel rule."

12. T. V. Bulpin, *Storm over the Transvaal* (Cape Town: Standard Press, 1955), p. 142. Kuper attributes this persistent strain of passivity toward the Europeans to a well-publicized dream of Sobhuza I foretelling of the power and irresistibility of the newcomers (*An African Aristocracy*, p. 19).

13. Estimates run between one-third and three-fourths of the total area: King Sobhuza II, "Petition of King Sobhuza II to the British Government Concerning Mineral Rights" (mimeographed, Lobamba, 1941), p. 2.

and as intense speculative fever swept Swaziland, the concessions increased. Mbandzeni became so alarmed that he again sought the aid of the British. Sir Theophilus Shepstone was now secretary of native affairs in Natal and sent his son, Theophilus Shepstone, Jr., better known as Offy. Offy was not an official of the British government, although there is evidence that the Swazis felt he was. He was also in a curious position. His chief purpose was to help Mbandzeni sort out and reduce the vast numbers of concessions; at the same time, he was to be paid for his trouble out of the revenues generated by the granting of *new* concessions. His task was further complicated by the size of the permanent European population in Swaziland (over 800), who tenaciously fought Offy's efforts to solve the problems generated by the concessions.

In addition, the South African Republic had long desired a port and were now thinking in terms of Kosi Bay on the Indian Ocean, the path to which lay through Swaziland. When Offy was dismissed in 1888 for refusing to register a concession, he turned to President Paul Kruger of the South African Republic for aid. Kruger, in turn, requested that a joint Boer-British committee be appointed to sort out the concessions. The British were not enthusiastic about the prospects of greater involvement in Swaziland. When Mbandzeni died that year and the queen regent, Labotshibeni (often known as Gwamile), reinstated Offy, they considered the matter at an end. But Boer interest in a path to the sea continued and at least one British representative in the republic, Sir Francis de Wenton, favored Boer involvement in Swaziland in preference to their designs on the territory north of the Limpopo.[14]

Seemingly in response to this view, President Kruger offered on May 3, 1889, to withdraw the republic's claim to the territory north of the Limpopo in exchange for Boer control over Swaziland and a corridor to the sea. The two governments then signed the Swaziland Convention of August 1890 by

14. Great Britain, Commonwealth Relations Office, *Swaziland, 1961* (London: Her Majesty's Stationery Office, 1962), p. 98. The interesting and complicated story of Boer desires for a route to the sea and British movements to thwart those ambitions is told in Noel Garson, *The Swaziland Question and the Road to the Sea, 1887-1895* (Johannesburg: University of Witwatersrand Press, 1957).

which the republic was allowed to annex the neighboring
Little Free State. As for the matter of a corridor to the sea,
the British were more than a little vague. "The point is that
the initiative was left to the Republic which was to conclude
treaties with Zambaan, Umbegisa and the Swazi for railway
strips and with the Tonga for a further strip and harbor
site." [15] The British did not mention that they were already
in consultation with several of these groups concerning eventual British protection over them. The Boers were apparently
not aware of these initiatives and during 1893 pressed for another Swaziland convention that would give them administrative jurisdiction over Swaziland. Britain signed the convention
but included a clause providing for Swazi approval. When the
Swazis refused to do so, Britain and the Republic signed a new
Swaziland Convention in 1894 that did not require Swazi acceptance. The Swazis protested vigorously and dispatched a
delegation to see Queen Victoria, who in turn refused to meet
with them, claiming they were now subject to Boer jurisdiction.

The British lost no time in undercutting the advantages
accruing to the Boers as the result of their take-over of Swaziland. On April 23, 1895, the British authorities in Natal annexed the domains of Zambaan and Umbegisa and, on May
30, established a protectorate over Tongaland, thereby sealing
off the Boers from the sea. The Boers were irritated over what
they took to be duplicity, although the abortive Jameson raid
of the same year overshadowed events in Swaziland.

In Swaziland a new ngwenyama, Bhunu (officially known as
Ngwane IV), was installed in 1894. He soon began a series of
purges which culminated in the killing of his principal governor, Mbabha Nsibande. The Boer administration summoned
him to Bremersdorp (now Manzini) to stand trial for murder.
Bhunu arrived, but with nearly 10,000 armed warriors. The
Boers were forced to send off to the republic for reinforce-
ments. When these arrived, complete with artillery, Bhunu
fled to Natal where he sought British protection and claimed
he could not be tried under the existing convention. Whether
out of conviction or spite, the British authorities declared that

15. Garson, p. 328. The siSwati spelling is "Sambane" and "Mbikiza."

Bhunu could not be tried: "there is no power in the Swaziland Convention of 1894 to try Ubunu in any court created under that convention." [16] Nevertheless, when the Boers offered to reduce the charges and guarantee his safety, the British convinced Bhunu to stand trial. He was found guilty of encouraging public violence and fined.[17] More importantly, the British and the Boers issued a joint protocol that removed criminal jurisdiction from the Swazi authorities.

The Boer administration of Swaziland from 1895 until the outbreak of the Anglo-Boer war was undistinguished save for some Swazi resistance to a newly imposed hut tax. When war came on October 1, 1899, the Boers withdrew from Swaziland. Bhunu used the opportunity to settle many old political scores and major bloodletting was terminated only by his death in December 1899. The Dlamini family council chose the grandson of Labotshibeni, Mona, to be the next ngwenyama, with Labotshibeni continuing as queen regent assisted by Mona's granduncle, Logqogqo, and Jokovu. After being educated at the Swazi school at Zombodze and Lovedale Institute in South Africa (1916–1919), Mona was installed in 1921 as Sobhuza II.

Following the Anglo-Boer War, the British assumed international responsibility for Swaziland and moved the capital from Bremersdorp to Mbabane. In 1903 control over Swaziland was vested in the governor of the Transvaal; but when the Transvaal attained self-government in 1906, control passed to the British high commissioner in South Africa. In 1907 more extensive administration was set up, with responsibility resting with the high commissioner for Swaziland, Basutoland, and the Bechuanaland Protectorate, but with three resident commissioners for each of the three areas. Each resident commissioner was assisted by the government secretary and six district commissioners. For most of the period 1906–1963, the high commissioner was merely a second hat worn by the British High Commission to the Union (and later, Republic) of South Africa. In 1963 the British government abolished the post of high commissioner and each of the resident commis-

16. Sobhuza II, "Petition," p. 9.
17. Dudley Barker, *Swaziland* (London: Her Majesty's Stationery Office, 1965), p. 36.

sioners became known as "Her Majesty's Commissioners."

Generally speaking, the British administration in Swaziland did not fully practice their celebrated policy of indirect rule. Because of the large number of European settlers, the fact that criminal jurisdiction had already been withdrawn from the Swazi king and because it was expected that Swaziland would eventually be incorporated into the Union of South Africa, a type of dual rule developed. The British administrators set up a national police force (1907) and contented themselves with issuing proclamations and enforcing them directly. Although they often consulted with the Swazi king, in effect the traditional Swazi authorities had their political power curtailed and their official responsibilities limited to the collection of taxes. It was not until World War II that the British belatedly set up a more conventional form of indirect rule for the Swazis. This meant that when decolonization did occur, the Swazi traditions had not been sullied by too close a collaboration with the British administration and therefore had more political options than their counterparts elsewhere in Africa.

Although provision was made in the South African Act of Union of 1909 for the eventual incorporation of the three High Commission territories into the union, the British government stipulated that the protected peoples of the three territories should have the final say concerning if and when such absorption would take place. South African attempts to incorporate Swaziland—most notably in 1913, 1927, 1933, 1935, and 1937—were turned down. The long and arduous record of this aspect of the history of Swaziland has been handled elsewhere.[18] Suffice it to say here that, with the coming to power

18. This topic has been the subject of extensive and often contradictory scholarship. Among the most widely read are Sir Charles Arden-Clarke, "The Problem of the High Commission Territories," *Optima* 8, no. 4 (December 1958): 163–170; G. V. Doxey, *The High Commission Territories and the Republic of South Africa* (Oxford: Oxford University Press, 1963); Sir Charles Dundas and Hugh Ashton, *Problem Territories of Southern Africa* (Johannesburg: South African Institute of International Affairs, 1952); Great Britain, *Basutoland, the Bechuanaland Protectorate, and Swaziland: History of Discussions with the Union of South Africa, 1909–1939* (London: His Majesty's Stationery Office, 1952); Jack Halpern, *South Africa's Hostages: Basutoland, Bechuanaland, and Swaziland* (Baltimore:

of the National Party in South Africa in 1948 and the increasing implementation of apartheid thereafter, the government of Great Britain gave up any thought of encouraging the inhabitants of the protectorate to accept union with South Africa and finalized this decision by removing the territories from jurisdiction of the Commonwealth Relations Office and placing them in the charge of the Colonial Office, under whose auspices they would eventually achieve independence.

Upon assuming responsibility for Swaziland, the British administration did attempt to evolve a coherent policy out of the concessionary morass. European grazing land, Swazi national land, European farms, Swazi homesteads—all were arrayed side by side. In addition to being residentially interspersed, the European and Swazi holdings often overlapped. A European might hold grazing rights to land already occupied by a number of Swazi farmers, while their claims might be further compromised by a third party holding the right to mineral development. A special committee was formed in 1904 to sort out the claims and spent two years doing so. Its findings were released in the Swaziland Concessions Partition Proclamation 28 of 1907, which empowered a special commissioner to divide the land officially into white, Swazi, and Crown land areas. In order to ensure that the Swazis received additional areas, he was to confiscate up to one-third of all concessions and return at least one-third of the land of Swaziland to the Swazis.

Whatever the intentions of the special commissioner and the problems of dealing with such a chaotic situation, the Swazis were dismayed when the delineation was over to find themselves separated into thirty-one different reserves with a total area of just over one-third of the country. Angry and

Penguin, 1965); Lord Hailey, *The Republic of South Africa and the High Commission Territories* (London: Oxford University Press, 1963); Margery Perham and Lionel Curtis, *The Protectorates of South Africa* (London: Oxford University Press, 1935); R. P. Stevens, *Lesotho, Botswana, and Swaziland: The Former High Commission Territories in Southern Africa* (New York: Praeger, 1967); and the Government of South Africa, *Negotiations Regarding the Transfer to the Union of the Government of Basutoland, the Bechuanaland Protectorate, and Swaziland, 1910–1939* (Pretoria: Government Printer, 1953).

frustrated, the Swazis sent a deputation to London in the same year, asking that the concession areas be reduced and the land returned to the Swazi nation. Although the British subsequently spent over $120,000 to reduce the concessionary holdings, the confiscated land did not accrue immediately to the Swazi nation.[19] Instead, the British government added the new areas to the existing Crown lands which the British had acquired as a result of the Anglo-Boer War. Deciding that further protests by her would be futile, Queen Mother Labotshibeni encouraged the Swazis to go to work in the mines in South Africa in order to repurchase their lost lands. Later, the new ngwenyama instituted a number of petitions for the recovery of land and mineral rights. He was not successful, however, and the issue of land reclamation and compensation remained with the Swazis until after their independence in 1968.

The story of the British administration during the 1920s and 1930s is quickly told, for as a high commissioner of that period wrote, "We might confine ourselves to doing as little in the way of administration . . . as possible." [20] A white advisory council was reestablished in 1921 to consult with the British administration on European affairs, but it soon lapsed into insignificance. Outside of a visit in 1927 by Secretary of State for the Dominions L. S. Amery, which led to the establishment of a land and agriculture fund, and a visit in 1932 by Sir Alan W. Pim, whose report led to the beginnings of British grants-in-aid to Swaziland, little was done.[21]

This brief summary of events in the history of pre–World War II Swaziland is designed to set the framework for an appreciation of traditional culture and its concomitant political system; for faced with the exogenous intrusions outlined above, it is important to explain how and why the Swazi nation was able to remain intact. It is to this analysis that we now turn. We are most fortunate to have the benefit of a great deal of

19. Hailey, *Native Administration*, p. 374.

20. Ben Cockram, "The Protectorates: An International Problem," *Optima* 13, no. 4 (December 1963): 21.

21. Sir Alan W. Pim, "Question of the South African Protectorates," *International Affairs* 13, no. 3 (September 1934): 668–688; and Government of Great Britain, *Cmnd. No. 4114* (London: His Majesty's Stationery Office, 1932).

material accumulated by the anthropologist Hilda Kuper and the British official Brian Marwick.[22] Although most of their research was conducted during the 1930s and 1940s, their observations are of great importance in understanding the events of the 1950s and 1960s, as well as the preceding decades.

General Cultural Patterns

In terms of basic societal patterns, the Swazi are similar to other southeastern Bantu-speaking groups, such as the Zulu. They fall into the general category that Melville J. Herskovits has termed the "East African cattle culture area." [23] For, as the Swazis told Kuper, "Cattle are our life, our bank, the property which establishes us." [24] Although the cattle play important economic, social, and cultural roles, the Swazis depend on subsistence agriculture for their food, with each family unit having its individual garden plots while sharing communal grazing land.[25]

The basic unit of Swazi society is the homestead, which includes an extended family under the leadership of a headman (*umnumzane*). Surrounding the cattle pen, or kraal, are the

22. In addition to using the Hilda Kuper books mentioned in n. 6, above, the following analysis is drawn from her *The Uniform of Color* (Johannesburg: University of Witwatersrand Press, 1947); idem, "The Swazi of Swaziland," in J. L. Gibbs (ed.), *Peoples of Africa* (New York: Holt, Rinehart, and Winston, 1965), pp. 479–512; idem, *Bite of Hunger* (New York: Harcourt, Brace and World, 1965); idem, *A Witch in My Heart* (London: Oxford University Press, 1970); Brian Marwick, *Abantu Bakwa Ngwane* (Cape Town: University of Cape Town Press, 1939); idem, *The Swazi* (Cambridge: Cambridge University Press, 1940); and Allister Miller, *Mamisa: The Swazi Warrior* (Pietermaritzburg: Shuter and Shuter, 1953). For a linguistic examination of siSwati, the interested reader should see the two works of Dirk Ziervogel, *A Grammar of Swazi* (Johannesburg: University of Witwatersrand Press, 1952), and *Swazi Texts* (Pretoria: Van Schaik, 1957); J. A. Engelbrecht, *Swazi Texts with Notes* (Cape Town: Nasionale Pers, 1930); and J. W. Arnheim, *Swaziland: A Bibliography* (Cape Town: School of Librarianship, 1950). The most satisfactory and up-to-date bibliography dealing with Swaziland is John B. Webster and Paulus Mohome, *A Bibliography on Swaziland* (Syracuse: Maxwell School of Citizenship and Public Affairs, 1968).

23. Melville J. Herskovits, *The Human Factor in Changing Africa* (New York: Knopf, 1962), pp. 62–79.

24. Kuper, *An African Aristocracy*, p. 150; Marwick, *The Swazi*, p. 179.

25. Sonja Jones, *A Study of Swazi Nutrition* (Durban: University of Natal Press, 1963).

living quarters of the family with separate sleeping facilities
for the head of the family's wife (or wives), for his mother,
and for the children and adolescents. The Swazis are patri-
lineal and patrilocal, although despite this male orientation
to Swazi society, there has always been a tradition that under-
scores the importance of woman. This is due in part to the
prestige enjoyed by the queen mother, the ndlovukazi, who is
the mother of the ngwenyama and his co-ruler: "The laws and
customs of the Swazi provide that every kraal shall be under
the joint control of mother and son. It is not the man and his
principal wife who run the affairs of a Swazi kraal; it must
be the man and his mother." [26]

The Swazi are connected by the web of kinship. There is
a rough hierarchy of seventy clans and numerous lineages, led
by the royal Nkosi Dlaminis, but this arrangement is "neither
precise nor static. While some clans have risen in rank through
diplomacy or loyalty, others have been degraded through con-
quest or the treachery of their representatives." [27] Even during
the middle of the nineteenth century, Swazi society was not
static. There were no hereditary jobs, no caste system, no im-
mutable aristocracy. In fact, one of the central features of the
Swazi monarchy was its provision for careers open to talented
commoners. The twentieth century, moreover, has seen substantial improvement in the upward mobility of individuals
due to the thrust of modernity in both the economic and political spheres, although the impact of this process should not
be exaggerated.

Land is of critical importance to the Swazis. All Swazi national land is vested in the ngwenyama, and theoretically he
can do with it "as he pleases." [28] In actuality, the rights to

26. Marwick, *The Swazi*, p. 65. Hilda Kuper found that only 17 percent
of the Swazi families were polygamous in the late 1940s and the number
has declined since then (*African Aristocracy*, p. 37). For some observations
on the dynamics of Swazi society, see A. R. Radcliffe-Brown and Daryll
Forde (eds.), *African Systems of Kinship and Marriage* (London: Oxford
University Press, 1950), pp. 80, 83, as well as Hilda Kuper, "Kinship
Among the Swazi," pp. 86–110, in the same volume.

27. Kuper, *An African Aristocracy*, p. 113; Dorothy Doveton, *The Human Geography of Swaziland* (London: George Philip and Son, 1937); and
idem, "Economic Geography of Swaziland," *Geographical Journal* 65, no.
3 (October 1936): 322–331.

28. Marwick, *The Swazi*, p. 158.

land use and its disposition are complicated, and the ngwenyama usually distributes the right to grant the use of land to
its chiefs of Swaziland who, in turn, assign it to their followers.
Before an individual can acquire the right to use land, he must
be officially recognized as a subject of the chief under whose
domain the land falls. "This membership can be acquired in
one of two ways; by being born into the Chiefdom, or by the
process known as *kukhonta,* offering allegiance to a Chief and
being accepted as his subject. It can also be lost (with the con-
sequent loss of all residential and land rights), either by ban-
ishment, or if a man voluntarily moves and settles in another
Chiefdom." [29]

In 1969, 44.71 percent of the land of Swaziland was held on
an individual basis with all but 1.2 percent of that freehold
land owned by whites.[30] This has led to local overcrowding
in the Swazi areas and a desire on the part of the Swazi leadership to receive compensation for the land alienated during
the past hundred years. On the theory that Great Britain, as
the colonial power, accepted and sanctified the European occupation, numerous Swazi delegations, the most recent in 1969,
have sought to have the government of Great Britain repay
the Swazi nation for its loss. The land issue also remains an
important factor in the domestic politics of Swaziland; for during the elections of 1964 and 1967, there were numerous complaints by the other parties that a number of chiefs had threatened to revoke the right to use land if their followers did not
support the Imbokodvo National Movement.

In Swazi society, it is the ngwenyama and the ndlovukazi
who provide the central symbolic referents for the life of the
nation. Although the Swazis believe in a supreme being, the
Mkhulumngqandi, he is remote, far removed from the lives

29. A. J. B. Hughes, *Swazi Land Tenure* (Natal: Institute for Social
Research, University of Natal, 1964), pp. 102, 202–271; and idem, "Some
Swazi Views on Land Tenure," *Africa: Journal of the International In-
stitute* 32, no. 3 (July 1962): 253–278.

30. G. M. E. Leistner and P. Smit, *Swaziland: Resources and Development* (Pretoria: African Institute of South Africa, 1969), p. 24. In 1968,
51.84 percent of the land of Swaziland was in communal use by the Swazis
and 3.45 percent was classified as Swazi National Land (this was formerly
Crown Land but now is in the process of being redistributed to the
Swazis).

of individuals. There is no class of priests among the Swazi, no sacred literature, and no religious orders, although the spirit world and the commonsensical one exist together on a space-time continuum and spirits are often consulted. Seeking cause and effect in a world inhabited in part by spirits, rural Swazis often attribute misfortune and calamity to the machinations of the unclean (who cause trouble without knowing it) and witches (who cause trouble out of spite). To combat these influences, there are diviners, magico-religious personages who "smell out" the evil doers. In former times, the miscreants were killed; now they are ostracized. There are also herbalists who use magic in an attempt to cure ailments but base their craft on a knowledge of medicinal roots and herbs.

The Traditional Swazi Political System

From the early part of the nineteenth century, the traditional Swazi political system was that of a powerful, centralized dual monarchy, headed by the ngwenyama and the ndlovukazi. Membership in the nation and in the political system was contingent on one's direct allegiance to the king. In a perceptive essay, S. N. Eisenstadt attempted to compare traditional political systems by examining the degree to which power diffusion takes place within them, their membership qualifications, and their relative amounts of subgroup autonomy.[31] The centralized monarchy is distinguished by a strong central political administration, heterogeneous membership, and hierarchical power configurations within the national unit. Membership in the polity is based not solely on kinship but on direct allegiance to the monarch. There are age-sets that further cut across clan and regional lines and promote political socializa-

31. S. N. Eisenstadt, "Primitive Political Systems: A Preliminary Comparative Analysis," *American Anthropologist* 61 (1959): 200–220. Other important attempts to compare traditional African political systems include E. E. Evans-Pritchard and M. Fortes (eds.), *African Political Systems;* Lucy Mair, *Primitive Government* (Baltimore: Penguin, 1962); I. Schapera, *Government and Politics in Tribal Societies* (London: Watts, 1956); Max Gluckman, *Politics, Law and Ritual in Tribal Societies* (Chicago: Aldine, 1965); Jan van Velsen, *The Politics of Kinship* (Manchester: Manchester University Press, 1967); and Jan Vansina, *Kingdoms of the Savanna* (Madison: University of Wisconsin Press, 1966).

tion and allegiance to the ruler. Thus, the Swazi political system is similar to that of the Zulu but differs markedly from those examples of the federated monarchies—such as the Ashanti, Xhosa, and Bembe—which have no age-regiments, greater subgroup autonomy, and less power in the hands of the central authority. This differentiation is further underscored by the fact that one's membership in the political community of a federated monarchy is dependent on one's prior membership in one of the subgroups.

These differences were to prove of enormous consequence in the 1950s and 1960s, for the traditional Swazi political system had long been able to absorb commoners and even non-Swazis into the political culture and to integrate them into the Swazi nation. This ability undoubtedly gave the Swazi traditional authorities a means of rejuvenating their system in modern times; and by demanding loyalty to the ngwenyama as the sine qua non of integration, large numbers of urbanized Swazis, non-Swazi Africans, and Europeans were able to be absorbed. Although the last two decades of political development in Swaziland include a variety of themes, one of the most persistent is the expansion of the traditional political system to include under its jurisdiction all elements of the population found within the borders of present-day Swaziland. The fact that modern political forms and institutional frameworks provided the mechanisms should not obscure the fact that the Swazi political system already contained the traditions and techniques that were to enable its leaders to utilize these new political inputs.

At the center of the traditional political system stand the dual monarchs, the ngwenyama (the Lion, the Sun, the Milky Way) and the ndlovukazi (the She Elephant, the Earth, the Bringer of Rains). In theory they are coequal. In practice, particularly since the reign of Sobhuza II, the ngwenyama is clearly the dominant force, although both are repositories of Swazi national law and custom and both have their own capitals and avenues of appeal for their subjects. The ndlovukazi is, however, of great importance during the transition from one ruler to the next, since succession is not by primogeniture. The heir to the throne is not known during the lifetime of the ngwenyama, although the king may advise a few close confidants of his preference. Upon his death, the ndlovukazi and the dead ngwenyama's senior paternal uncles call a Dlamini family council (*Lusendvo*) to choose a successor. They are required by customary law only to select the only son of the dead king's "favorite" wife, "favorite" being broadly interpreted depending on circumstance but generally associated with her clan rank. The "favorite" wife then rules in conjunction with the ndlovukazi until the young prince comes of age and his mother becomes the new ndlovukazi. For example, Labotshibeni acted as regent (1899–1921) during the minority of young Mona who became Sobhuza II. After Sobhuza II was installed, his own mother, Lomawa, became the ndlovukazi in 1925 following the death of Labotshibeni. The nation cannot be without an ndlovukazi so that should she die before her son, one of her co-sisters is selected to be the substituted ndlovukazi. (Sobhuza's mother died in 1938; her sister Nukwase replaced her.)

As powerful as the Swazi monarchy is, however, it is not absolute. There are two major institutions to which it is responsible and which also serve to integrate the polity. The first and most important is the Swazi *Liqoqo*, or Inner Council, which consists of a small group of between twenty and thirty chiefs and commoners who regularly consult with the ngwenyama. He is expected to confer with its members on all matters of state and to take advice from it. Within the confines of the council, the king debates on a more or less equal basis with the other members. When the matter is decided and fully accepted in the Liqoqo (no vote is taken), the issue is announced to the nation as a command from the king. In recent years, many of its functions have been taken over by an executive committee of the larger Swazi National Council (*Libandla laka Ngwane*) known as the *Libandla 'ncane*, or Little Council.[32] The Libandla 'ncane consists of many members of the Liqoqo but with a number of appointees of the ngwenyama, often government officials with "modern" expertise, since the Libandla 'ncane is more often concerned with affairs dealing with the country of Swaziland (often economic

32. Hughes, *Swazi Land Tenure*, p. 137.

matters) rather than matters dealing with the Swazi cultural nation. The Swazi National Council, or Libandla laka Ngwane, is a general meeting of chiefs and headmen open to all adult males who have been born or accepted into the Swazi nation. Anyone present may speak in its meetings, and again no formal votes are taken. It is seldom called, and its large size and infrequent operations make it essentially a mechanism by which the ngwenyama and the Liqoqo can convey to the population at large the issues facing them. Local dissemination of decisions taken by the political center are usually transmitted to the rural population by the Liqoqo as well as by the bureaucracy. Even today, information concerning bills passed by the national Parliament often are carried to the people in this way.

The ngwenyama stands at the head of an extensive bureaucracy, which consists of princes of the realm, some without chieftaincies of their own, and the appointed *tindvuna* who may be of noble or common birth.[33] They have both civil and quasi-military functions and are directly responsible to the ngwenyama. They traditionally served as "his eyes and ears" to provide an ongoing check on, and serve as intermediators with, the local chiefs. In choosing the tindvuna, the king must strike a balance between appointments of birth and appointments of merit and "The king is careful not to give too much power to male kinsmen and certain highly coveted administrative posts are monopolized by commoners."[34] The local chiefs have more autonomy. Swazi national area is divided into districts, each headed by a chief (*sikhulu*) who has control over membership in the local community and the power of land allocation. The chiefs also have their own tindvuna and local versions of the Liqoqo. The royal bureaucracy is a distinguishing feature of the centralized monarchy and has been of great importance in enabling the Swazi kings not only to aid in national integration by curbing potential dysfunctional regional forces but also to provide the political system

33. The *tindvuna* are not to be confused with the ritual blood brothers of the ngwenyama, the *tinsila,* who are commoners chosen to protect the king from his male kinsmen and whose function is now largely ceremonial.

34. Kuper, *An African Aristocracy,* p. 60.

with important channels of upward mobility. The tradition of "careers open to talent," dependent only on expertise and loyalty to the ngwenyama, was to serve the Swazi political system in good stead, since erstwhile opponents of the monarchy were later accepted back into the political fold through this device; it would not be farfetched to see the appointed seats in the House of Assembly and Senate as logical extensions of this pattern and as a vital means of integrating non-Swazis into the newly enlarged political system.

The Swazi traditional political system has also made use of the Zulu-inspired age-set system (*emabutfho*) introduced by Mswati to inculcate the ideal of citizenship, loyalty to the ngwenyama and the Swazi nation. Each *lifbutfho*, or regiment, consists of all able-bodied men of the same age who are brought together during adolescence for training and education of a social as well as a political nature: "Here each member of the regiment is educated as to his responsibilities to his seniors and his rights with regard to his juniors." [35] Each regiment has its own living quarters, songs, and insignia and is under the leadership of a prince and a commoner, both appointed by the ngwenyama. A new regiment is formed when the majority of men in the preceding one become married. During 1969, two new regiments were formed, the *Inkhanyeti*, or "Star," regiment for men under fifteen and the *Gcina*, or "End of an Era," regiment for men from the ages of fifteen to twenty-five. During the nineteenth century, the regiments served not only as an institution of socialization but also provided the Swazi leaders with military formations. Today, the emabutfho are more like a national service corps. While a particular regiment is in training, it is divided into smaller units and given various chores such as weeding or harvesting the royal plots or some other public works project. Once the regiment completes its cycle, it is dismissed and is called up only for ceremonial purposes and in times of national crisis. During 1965 and again during 1969, for example, the ngwen-

35. *Ibid.*, p. 127. A full description of the age-sets is found in *An African Aristocracy*, pp. 117–136, and in her "The Development of the Military Organization of Swaziland," *Africa* 10, no. 1 (1937): 55–74, and 10, no. 2 (1937): 176–205.

yama called on several regiments to combat the outbreak of
foot-and-mouth disease by aiding the national police in their
efforts to control movement to and from the infected areas. At
the same time, the regiments are not armed with modern weapons or trained in security procedures, so that they are virtually
powerless in a major crisis (such as the disorders of 1963).

The regiment system for women is less formal, and women
of the same age do not live apart in barracks but meet peri-
odically to learn the importance of various rituals as well as
their place in the Swazi community. They participate as a
group, however, in such yearly festivals as the reed dance.

There is a great deal of significance to the ritual role played
by the ngwenyama. He is more than a symbol of unity, for his
importance to the nation is constantly underscored by the
thoughts and actions of his subjects. He is expected to have
the largest cattle herds in the country, the most land under
cultivation, and the greatest number of wives. His residence,
cars, dogs, even his personal effects have special names. Nowhere is his importance to the nation seen more clearly than
in the most significant ritual occasion in the yearly Swazi
cycle, the annual *Incwala*. The Incwala ceremony is many
things. Brian Marwick saw it as primarily a first fruits ceremony, with economic and seasonal importance concerned with
the taboos and customs of harvest time.[36] Gwendolen Carter
viewed it in more national terms, feeling that it generated a
sense of solidarity among the Swazis.[37] Max Gluckman regarded it as at least in part an effort to influence "the uni-
verse." [38] Hilda Kuper perceived it as essentially an attempt
to perpetuate the glory of the ngwenyama and to demonstrate
the magical way in which the king is the nation and the nation
is the king.[39] In this latter regard, there are, for example, no

36. Marwick, *The Swazi*, pp. 182–195.

37. Gwendolen M. Carter, "Sacred Fertility Festival," *Africa Special
Report* 2, no. 4 (April 1957): 5.

38. Max Gluckman, *Politics, Law and Ritual in Tribal Societies* (Chicago: Aldine, 1965), p. 254.

39. Kuper, *African Aristocracy*, pp. 197–225. The description that fol-
lows is condensed from this section. Interesting comments on this important aspect of Swazi life are also found in Max Gluckman, *Rituals of
Rebellion* (Manchester: Manchester University Press, 1952).

full celebrations of the Incwala during the future king's minority, and no one except he may lead the ceremonies. It is of, by, and for him as the living embodiment of the Swazi nation.

The Incwala is broken into two parts and runs for an entire month, a two-day "little" Incwala and a six-day "big" Incwala, the former being in many ways a dress rehearsal of the latter. The little Incwala begins on the first moonless night after the winter solstice. Ritual specialists are sent out early in December to fetch water from the sea, timing their arrival for the beginning of the ceremony. The king's oldest regiment greets their arrival, and the ngwenyama comes to spit the sacred water to the east and west to signal the cutting off of the old year.

Two weeks later when the full moon rises, the big Incwala begins. "Pure," unmarried youths are sent to cut branches from a special shrub, *Lusekwane*. On the second day, they return and place the branches in a newly constructed sanctuary for the ngwenyama. During the third day, a black ox is turned loose in the enclosure and is beaten to death by the bare fists of the youths. The most significant day of the ceremony is the fourth, when in the presence of the regiments the ngwenyama banishes all royal Dlaminis and foreigners from the sanctuary and sings with his subjects, who in turn reaffirm their loyalty. With this action, the ngwenyama is rejuvenated, the Swazi nation is revitalized, and the new year can begin. On the fifth day, all is silent and the land remains in a state of limbo. On the sixth day, the king emerges from his sanctuary and lights a fire which burns until everything used in the ceremony is consumed. When the rains come, the first fruits of the harvest and the potency of the ngwenyama, his nation, and the land are assured and the new year can proceed.

Thus, the political power of the ngwenyama is strengthened by the tribal structure and its independent bureaucracy answerable to him, by the traditional pattern of decision making which involves the Liqoqo, by such socializing institutions as the embutfho, and by the ongoing ritual of the nation. Interestingly enough, the anthropological studies of the 1930s and 1940s tended to view the Swazis as a conservative, tradition-bound people, who were about to enter a transitional stage that would cause the breakdown of traditional authority and the disintegration of the tribal unit. In short, it seemed unlikely that the Swazi traditional authorities would survive as a potent political force in the face of decolonization, economic development, and the emergence of modern national politics. Yet, as matters turned out, the Swazi political system had within itself the possibility of rejuvenation, and its leaders were constantly buoyed by the cohesion of its culture. A national unit that had held together through a century of partition, division, and colonial control was not about to collapse in the face of intrusions of modern political philosophies and techniques. As the remainder of this study indicates, the traditional elite not only did not lose control over the existing cultural nation but, in fact, markedly increased its power. By using the intrusion of modernity (in the form of large-scale economic projects, a series of Westminster-type constitutions, and national parties) to their own advantage, the traditional authorities proved to be both resilient and adaptive. In addition, the traditional authorities acted in such a way as to promote political development. The monarchy in particular played an important role in stimulating activities often associated with political modernization: the development of an institutional matrix for the entire country, greatly increased political participation, the creation of effective linkages between the central political authority and its constituents, and the political integration of the entire country.

This is not to say that Sobhuza II deliberately set out to lead his people to political modernity. He emphatically did not, for initially he accepted the premise that any increase in political activity and any changes in the authority patterns of the political system would threaten his position. It was not until he was confronted by the colonial authority and the modern political parties that he reacted. Thus, his activities more than his designs led to political development. However, his reaction set in motion, and his success ensured, that aspects of political modernization would become facts of life in Swaziland. Few would have predicted this course of events. Both the colonial authority and the leaders of the modern political parties long argued that the direct involvement of the monarchy in political competition would dilute the power and prestige of his position and might even fragment the polity. This view was not proven by subsequent events. Sobhuza II emerged more powerful than any Swazi ruler since Mswati and, in terms of enlarging the scope of his domain to include non-Swazis, the most powerful ruler in the history of the nation. One should not attempt to generalize about the survival of traditional authorities on the basis of this unique situation, but the Swazi experience does indicate that modernity does not, ipso facto, mean the destruction or dilution of their power even though in most recent African cases this has been the result.

2

The Thrust of Modernity

THE SOCIOECONOMIC SITUATION IN SWAZILAND FOLLOW-
ing World War II hardly seemed propitious for economic or
political development. The country had remained for three decades in one of the backwaters of Britain's African empire, and
the dimensions of its stagnation were considerable. In the first
place, physical infrastructure was rudimentary at best. There
were no tarred roads, no railroads, no airports in the entire
country, so that, depending on the season and the weather,
travel was both difficult and hazardous. Supplies of water and
electricity were sporadic and undependable even in the principal population centers of Mbabane, Manzini, and Stegi (now
Siteki). Health conditions were generally poor. Malaria, tuberculosis, gastroenteritis, pneumonia, and malnutrition were
rampant. Infant mortality was as high in Swaziland as it was
anywhere in Africa.[1] There was one doctor for every twenty
thousand inhabitants. Medical facilities were rare and for the
most part confined to the urban areas.[2] Great portions of the
country were susceptible to outbreaks of hoof-and-mouth disease and attacks of *bovine trypanosoniasis*.

The economic situation was hardly more auspicious. Capital
was extremely scarce, and the cash sector of the economy was
very small including no more than 5 percent of the working-

1. Barker, *Swaziland*, p. 130. For a detailed examination of the incidence
rates of these afflictions, see the Government of Swaziland series, *Annual
Report of Medical and Sanitary Reports* (Mbabane: Government Printer,
1943, 1944, 1945, 1946, 1947). As late as 1960, average per capita calorie
intake by Swazis amounted to but 74 percent of the minimum daily re-
quirement (Jones, *A Study of Swazi Nutrition*, p. 135).
2. Kuper, *Uniform of Color*, p. 78.

age population. Most of the population existed as subsistence farmers and pastoralists. More than 8,000 Swazis, or fully 20 percent of the adult male labor force, were employed outside the country, primarily in South Africa.[3] The Havelock asbestos mine was the only large-scale industrial enterprise in the entire country, and in 1946 the value of its exports exceeded those of the next largest producer by 400 percent.[4] In addition, the concessionary period had left a depressing legacy that was a major impediment to economic development of any kind. Slightly more than 3 percent of the population, almost all of them Europeans, owned 42.5 percent of the land of Swaziland, while the other 97 percent of the population, primarily Swazi, owned but 52.5 percent of the land, with the remaining portions held by the British government.[5] While this pattern of land ownership in and by itself did not militate against economic development, there were further complications stemming from the overlapping and often conflicting rights to surface use and mineral exploitation. The rights to mineral development covering 48.9 percent of the country were held by European individuals and corporations, 2.8 percent by the Swazis, and 48.3 percent by the British government.[6] Often one individual would have the rights to mineral exploitation on a piece of property, while another had the rights to general land usage, and a third held grazing rights. Incredibly, rights to over 50,000 acres of the high and middle velds, almost 10 percent of the land of Swaziland, were held by South African ranchers for winter grazing of sheep from the Transvaal.[7] In addition to the conflicting patterns of land ownership and land

3. Government of Great Britain, Colonial Office, *Swaziland, 1946* (London: His Majesty's Stationery Office, 1948), p. 21.

4. *Ibid.*, p. 27.

5. European Advisory Council, "Minutes of the Reconstituted European Advisory Council 1945–1955" (mimeographed by the government secretary, Mbabane, 1955), p. 8.

6. H. J. R. Way, *Mineral Ownership as Affecting Mineral Development of Swaziland* (Mbabane: Government Printer, 1955), p. 11. Mineral concessions had lapsed to the Crown over the years because of nonconformation with the stipulations of the grants, cessation of operations, or voluntary surrender.

7. J. B. McI. Daniel, *Geography of the Rural Economy of Swaziland* (Durban: University of Natal Press, 1962), p. 188.

use, there was a serious lack of knowledge about the possibilities of economic development. There were, for example, no mineral surveys available for the entire country, no coherent plan for economic development. Until these were forthcoming, the concessions sorted out, and sufficient amounts of capital procured, economic development would remain a distant dream.

There were other problems of a socioeconomic nature as well. Education, for example, was in a deplorable state; in 1946 only 12 percent of the European children and 6 percent of the Swazi were enrolled in territorial schools of any kind.[8] In fact, there was no organized, coherent school system encompassing the entire territory, and whatever government funds were allocated to the various mission-sponsored and Swazi national schools were dispersed on a segregated, highly inequitable basis.

In fact, a pervasive pattern of social and economic discrimination was discernible in all areas of daily life in Swaziland. Africans living in the territory were subject to a number of common injustices, which ranged from being denied access to many public establishments to wage differentials that were often on the order of ten to one. The national police force was dominated by Europeans. The entire officer corps was white and the ready reserve, drawn from the various rifle clubs in Swaziland, did not have any African members at all, regardless of position.[9] Similar discriminatory patterns existed in private industry, commerce, and government service.

It is against this background that the major thrust of economic and political modernity into Swaziland occurred during the 1950s and early 1960s; it was to change the course of the country's future. This is not to say that the influences I shall

8. Government of Swaziland, *Annual Report of the Department of Education, 1946* (Mbabane: Government Printer, 1948), p. 19. In Basutoland (now Lesotho) 200 miles to the southwest, the corresponding figure was 85 percent for the African population (Hailey, *Native Administration*, p. 404).

9. The British government maintained that the membership of the clubs was "voluntarily confined to European male residents of Swaziland" (Government of Great Britain, Colonial Office, *Swaziland, 1956* [London: Her Majesty's Stationery Office, 1957], p. 59).

label "modern" were simply a product of the post–World War
II period; for the exogenous, primarily western European-
inspired changes in Swazi life had taken place gradually over
almost a century and a half. Rather, it is to indicate that the
tempo of such changes increased markedly during the period
under review, reaching a crescendo in the late 1950s and early
1960s, and began, for the first time, to touch on the lives of
most persons living in Swaziland. These changes were to alter
the character of Swazi national life substantially and to lead
to new economic and political configurations that would accompany the territory into the independence period.

For the sake of analytical simplification, I have organized
the heightened intrusion of modernity into two primary categories: physical-technical and administrative-political. In examining the phenomena that followed, it should be remembered that these two categories were not, in fact, discrete; they
often overlapped, combined, or were mutually interactive.
Furthermore, while the inputs into the territory were to have
a discernibly cumulative impact, they did not always follow as
coherent or direct a pattern as the following analysis might
suggest.

Physical and Technical Inputs

Two major sources of change in the post–World War II collective life of Swaziland were the advances of modern medicine
and the infusions of major amounts of venture capital, both
public and private, which were to make Swaziland one of the
healthiest and richest (as measured by per capita income) countries in Africa. Also, taken together, these two categories of influence were to produce major demographic and economic
changes which ultimately were to have important political
ramifications, not only for the internal dynamics of politics in
Swaziland but also for the entire interstate subsystem of Southern Africa. Thus, economic development, while it was ultimately to increase the distributive capability of the independence government, was also to limit the government's range of
political options vis-à-vis the Republic of South Africa and the
Portuguese-controlled area of Mozambique.

One important change, illustrative of the importation and

implementation of medical technology, was the suppression of malaria. Until World War II, malaria covered most of Swaziland east of the high veld and was a major drag on economic development, since it caused widespread disability among Swazis and discouraged European settlement and entrepreneurship in many parts of the territory. A government survey conducted during the period from 1947 until 1949 indicated the feasibility of a malaria eradication program. Thereafter, the colonial administration allocated substantial funds, often totaling 8 to 10 percent of the territorial budget from 1950 until 1957. By 1959 the threat of malaria had been virtually eliminated and the governmental health services could turn their attention to other serious health problems such as malnutrition and tuberculosis.[10] It is hoped that this one example will suffice to indicate the direction of change during the postwar period, for it would not be going too far to say that the medical advances of the 1950s were extremely important in setting the stage for many of the economic developments that were to follow in that they encouraged permanent settlement and capital investment and generally improved the quality of life in the territory. At the very least, they signaled a greater interest on the part of the colonial authority in the physical well-being of the citizens of the territory.

Of greater direct consequence for the economic development of Swaziland was the dramatic rise in the rate of capital investment within the country. While considerable amounts came from private sources, primarily from South Africa but also from Great Britain and the United States, the major impetus for economic development was provided by the British Colonial Development Corporation (CDC), later (1963) renamed the Commonwealth Development Corporation. The CDC was created by the British government to implement the Second Colonial Development and Welfare Act of 1945. In addition to providing the technical assistance for a number of economic surveys, the CDC became the primary underwriter for large-scale development projects such as plantation agriculture, irrigation schemes, and mineral extraction ventures. It

10. Government of Swaziland, *Annual Report of Medical and Sanitary Reports, 1959* (Mbabane: Government Printer, 1960), p. 3.

was also instrumental in the dramatic improvement in the physical infrastructure of Swaziland by developing the road network, by aiding in the creation of hydroelectric facilities, and by helping to underwrite the cost of the Swaziland railroad which was to run the length of the country. By borrowing money from the British government at a 3 percent interest rate, the CDC was able to make available considerable amounts of capital in support of many private ventures and to provide much needed organizational and technical skills for some of the larger projects. Eventually, this aid totaled nearly $70 million, a considerable amount for a country with a population of slightly more than 400,000 (by 1968).

Two of the CDC projects were to prove of particular importance in paving the way for Swaziland's economic takeoff: the forestry development plans in the high veld and the irrigation schemes in the middle and low velds. In 1943 the private firm of Swaziland Plantations began forestry planting on 3,500 acres near Piggs Peak; four years later Peak Timbers followed suit on a 30,000-acre tract. The trees, primarily *Pinus patula* and *Pinus elliottii,* grew so well and the world demand for timber and pulp products continued so strong that the CDC undertook to support a massive project of afforestation in the Usutu Valley. It sponsored the construction of roads, base camps, and a pulp mill that would utilize wood from both smaller plantations and the proposed new area. Eventually, Usutu Pulp became the largest manmade forest in Africa with a total area of over 90,000 acres. The production of forest products soon became one of the three major industries in the territory and, in the process, helped to make a railroad across the entire width of Swaziland economically feasible.

Of even greater consequence for the economic development of Swaziland were the efforts of the CDC to stimulate large-scale irrigation projects on the Komati and Usutu rivers. In contrast to the predominant role played by private investment in the development of a citrus fruit industry during the 1950s, it was CDC sponsorship that made sugar production economically viable. In the areas of low veld near Komati and Big Bend, the CDC provided technical assistance and financial support for hydroelectric projects, irrigation surveys, and the building of two mills to process the sugar. The sugar production facilities at Ubombo Ranches and Mhlume Sugar not only opened up heretofore underdeveloped portions of Swaziland (in the process, providing a far larger number of jobs than had previously been available to Swazis in the mines in South Africa), but also stimulated the entire economic life of the country. By 1966, over 50,000 acres were under irrigation, and the production of sugar became the largest yearly earner of export revenues. This trend continued into the 1970s. In addition, the consistent rate of traffic from the sugar mills, coupled with that generated by the forestry complexes and an iron ore mine, made the Swaziland railroad a reality and, in turn, helped to link Swaziland with the Indian Ocean port of Lourenço Marques.

In addition to the activities of the CDC, the British administration in Swaziland made a concerted effort to promote economic development by providing technical assistance, forward planning, and a series of economic overviews of the development potential of the country. To coordinate these activities, the government introduced an eight-year plan in 1948 and a five-year plan in 1955,[11] and established a natural resources board in December 1953. The following May, the government appointed a geologist to investigate the possibilities of using mineral extraction to spur the general economic growth of the territory. As a result of his findings, the government established a Swaziland Mineral Development Commission in October 1953 with the expressed function of analyzing the existing patterns of mineral development and concession holdings in order "to make recommendations as to how the latter may be simplified in the general interests of the Territory." [12] Following the report of the commission's findings, the government imposed a tax on all mineral concessions whether they were being used or not. Despite the opposition of most of the concession holders, the policy had the net effect of forcing

11. Government of Swaziland, *The Five-Year Development Plan Covering the Period 1 April 1955 to 31 March 1960* (Mbabane: Government Printer, 1954).

12. Government of Great Britain, *Official Gazette: Swaziland, 1953* (Mbabane: Government Printer, 1954), p. 67.

owners to develop their concessions or, because of the cost, to surrender them to the Crown which could then utilize the most promising. By 1961, mineral concessions covering 74.4 percent of the total land in Swaziland were in the hands of the government, thereby giving the CDC the opportunity to attract outside capital by offering large blocks of available land.[13] The extensive iron ore deposits at Bomvu ridge, for example, were found on Crown land.

It was, in fact, two government-sponsored surveys that indicated that approximately sixty million tons of high-grade ore existed at Bomvu northwest of Mbabane. Studies also suggested that extraction would be economically feasible if long-term contracts for its use could be found and suitable transportation facilities arranged.[14] Since the iron ore deposits were located approximately 150 miles from the Portuguese-controlled port of Lourenço Marques and 30 miles from the South African railhead at Barberton, extensive rail facilities would have to be built. A number of factors, including political ones, would enter into the subsequent decision concerning the direction of the ore flow, but it would be the arrangement of long-term ore contracts that would give the final impetus to the development of the Swaziland railroad.

Based on the demonstrator and pump-priming effects of the various CDC projects and a corresponding growth of private investment, the government felt that economic development was likely to be enduring and of such a character that it would draw into the cash sector of the economy large numbers of Swazis who would become members of a permanent work force or who would emerge as individual entrepreneurs, feeding their products into the primary product-processing facilities that were being established for the large-scale plantations. With this end in mind, the government initiated a number of breeding stations, demonstration plots, and other examples of

13. Government of Great Britain, Colonial Office, *Swaziland, 1961* (London: Her Majesty's Stationery Office, 1962), p. 44.

14. D. N. Davies and J. G. Urie, *The Bomvu Ridge Harmatite Deposits* (Mbabane: Government Printer, 1956). For a general introduction to the previous proposals for a railroad through Swaziland, see Alan C. G. Best, *The Swaziland Railway: A Study in Politico-Economic Geography* (East Lansing: Michigan State University Press, 1966), pp. 1–27.

modern farming techniques. In this endeavor, the administration and the ngwenyama often worked together, the king allowing the use of royal land or royal cattle and the British agricultural experts providing fertilizer and technical knowledge.

Despite good intentions, however, the record of the British government in general, and the CDC in particular, in drawing Swazi into modern economic life was not without ambiguity, especially in the immediate postwar period. During the 1940s, the government embarked on a modest program of land reform that was designed to purchase European-owned land for the eventual use of the Swazis. The Swazi leadership participated in this program by establishing the Lifa fund. The fund had a twofold purpose. It instituted a tax on Swazi-owned cattle in the hope that, as Swazis were forced to sell their cattle to pay the tax, overstocking in the Swazi areas would be gradually reduced. The money thus collected would be used by the Swazi nation to purchase the European-owned land. Although the project initially went well, it soon ran into difficulty. Rural Swazi showed a great reluctance to part with their cattle and deeply resented the tax. Then, there were some local scandals involving the misuse of tax funds. Finally, and most important, the local chiefs felt that the entire scheme was part of a government plot to undermine their authority over land allocation. Many Swazis were generally suspicious of the heightened European interest in Swazi cattle and land. For all these reasons, the Lifa fund was eventually abandoned, although it did have some initial success in reducing European portions of the land in Swaziland.[15]

For its part, the CDC did not always take the lead in stressing Swazi participation in its major projects and, in fact, seemed to be gearing much of its aid to the European sector of the economy. The CDC may have been seeking to ensure

15. By 1961 the fund was credited with the purchase of 268,000 acres (Government of Great Britain, Colonial Office, *Swaziland, 1961* [Mbabane: Government Printer, 1962], p. 28). The activities of the CDC are fully documented in Government of Swaziland, *Annual Report of the Colonial Development and Welfare Schemes: Estimates of Revenues and Expenditures* (Mbabane: Government Printer, 1957, 1958, 1959, 1960, 1961, 1962, 1963, 1964, 1965, 1966).

rapid economic growth and had seen the European community as the major repository for the entrepreneurial skills, matching capital, and willingness to attempt projects of the scale outlined above. Nevertheless, it seemed to the Swazis that funds for the various projects were accruing to the already (by Swazi standards at least) well-to-do Europeans. This, coupled with the fact that some CDC personnel were openly discriminatory in their dealings with the Swazis, helped to ensure that most Swazis did not see themselves as benefiting directly from the CDC's efforts. Curiously enough, many Europeans in the territory held the view that the CDC and the administration were working in collusion against the interests of those Europeans who held mineral concessions and were sacrificing European interests to those of the Swazis.[16] On balance, during the late 1940s and early 1950s, it would seem that the activities of the CDC, while ultimately economically constructive, were decisive in their impact on Swazi-European relations. This dual legacy would emerge during the political campaigns of 1964 and 1967. In subsequent chapters, I shall deal with this aspect of government-sponsored economic development, as well as with the question of why the CDC was to devote the bulk of funds earmarked for Southern Africa to Swaziland rather than to the far poorer territories of Basutoland and the Bechuanaland Protectorate. At this juncture, it should simply be pointed out that the surge in economic life and the enlargement of the cash sector of the economy that resulted from the CDC's efforts were to present the would-be political elites in the territory with both local prosperity and considerable socioeconomic problems as well as a generally improved standard of living by the time of independence in 1968.

Administrative and Political Inputs

If the immediate postwar period hastened the pace of economic development, it also brought with it far-reaching changes in the political structure of Swaziland. Although the decisive

16. The debates of the European Advisory Council are filled with acrimonious arguments, charges, and countercharges over this issue. See especially European Advisory Council, "Minutes of the Reconstituted Advisory Council" (mimeographed by the government secretary, Mbabane, 1954–1955, 1956).

events that were to lead Swaziland to independence did not occur until the mid-1960s, the initial framework within which they were to take place was established much earlier. In the late 1940s and early 1950s the British colonial authorities gave formal recognition to two groups—the elected leaders of the European community and the Swazi traditional hierarchy—which would ultimately influence the nature of the decolonization political framework of Swaziland. By reconstituting the European Advisory Council and redefining the position of the ngwenyama and the Swazi National Council, the British government provided both groups with political power, visibility, and the appearance of official sanction, so that, as new political forces emerged, they found themselves confronting deeply entrenched opposition.

The European community in Swaziland has always enjoyed a privileged position. As far back as 1888, the settlers obtained a charter of self-government from Mbandzeni. The all-white body formed subsequently, the European Advisory Council, played an important role in formulating and expressing European opinion during the rest of the nineteenth century. Racked by internal divisions, however, and reduced in importance as a result of the British take-over in 1903, it fell into disuse during the twentieth century.[17]

With the end of World War II and the subsequent emphasis on economic development, the British administration concluded that Europeans would have to play a more meaningful role in the collective life of the territory if development were to be forthcoming. In 1949, therefore, the administration moved to reconstitute the European Advisory Council to "advise the Resident Commissioner on matters specifically referred to the Council by the Resident Commissioner."[18] The Reconstituted European Advisory Council (REAC) consisted of ten elected members chosen by the Europeans in the territory, the deputy resident commissioner, and six senior government officials appointed by the Resident Commission, who led the dis-

17. The British government did accept its advisory status in 1921 but tended to bypass it whenever possible.
18. Government of Great Britain, Colonial Office, *Swaziland, 1949* (London: His Majesty's Stationery Office, 1950), p. 25.

cussions of the council. It seems clear that the British administration intended to limit the council to a purely advisory
role and to confine its activities to European problems; but as
matters turned out, this role was not what the European community had in mind.

For most of its institutional life, the REAC did not content
itself with remaining within the administration's guidelines; it
soon became a ready forum for European opinion on almost
any subject, an avenue of attack against the colonial adminis-
trations, and an opportunity for the Europeans to involve
themselves even more directly in the affairs of the Swazis. The
minutes of the REAC's proceedings, therefore, are filled with
lively, often acrimonious debates dealing with such questions
as land ownership, mineral development, citizenship, political
refugees, Swazi government, and ultimately constitutional advance.[19] Later, buoyed by support from the Swazi hierarchy,
the REAC tenaciously resisted the British vision for a nonracial one-man, one-vote political system; and until it was
superseded by the territorial-wide Legislative Council in June
1964, the REAC acted as a major blockage to political development as proposed by the British authorities.

In much the same fashion, the official recognition by the
British administration of the powers of the ngwenyama and
the restoration of some of the rights and prerogatives that had
been withdrawn from his office during the Boer occupation
were ultimately to thwart their constitutional proposals. As
indicated in chapter one, the British did not begin to follow
their conventional form of indirect rule with regard to the
Swazis until 1944, favoring, partially by design and partially
by default, a modified form of dual rule. In 1944, however,
by Proclamation 44 the administration recognized "the Paramount Chief and Council as the Native Authority for the
Territory and invested the Native Authority with power to
issue to Natives in Swaziland legally enforceable orders on a

19. Interested readers should consult the following: European Advisory
Council, "Minutes of the Reconstituted European Advisory Council"
(mimeographed by the government secretary, Mbabane, 1949–1950, 1950–
1953, 1954–1955, 1956, 1957, 1958, 1959, 1960, 1961, 1962, 1963, 1964).

sizeable number of subjects." [20] Proclamation 44 did not entirely rescue the ngwenyama from the limbo into which the European occupation had thrust his office, for, as a British spokesman was to declare, "The Nation has at no time participated in responsibility for public services to an extent comparable with the normal practice in dependent British territories in Africa." [21] Despite the validity of this observation, the British were unwilling to expand the powers of the ngwenyama at that time, despite the fact that Sobhuza II and the Swazi National Council immediately pressed for additional recognition of the ngwenyama's power and a return of his criminal jurisdiction.[22]

The reconstitution of the European Advisory Council, however, gave the Swazis a new bargaining point. After considerable pressure, the British issued three additional proclamations that formally restored many of the ngwenyama's more important powers. Proclamation 79 of 1950 recognized the ngwenyama as having the power to appoint chiefs and to issue legally enforceable orders to be published in the Official Gazette of the territory.[23] In a real sense, Proclamation 79 simply gave official administrative sanction to what was already a fact; but coming at this time, it seemed to commit the British authorities to the existing political order. At any rate, this is how the situation was viewed by the Swazi authorities, and they vigor-

20. Government of Great Britain, Colonial Office, *Swaziland, 1946* (London: His Majesty's Stationery Office, 1947), p. 50.

21. Government of Great Britain, Commonwealth Relations Office, *Basutoland, Bechuanaland Protectorate, and Swaziland: Report of an Economic Survey Mission* (London: Her Majesty's Stationery Office, 1960) p. 426.

22. Lord Hailey notes that during these discussions, the Swazis were well supported by European legal advisers, many from South Africa (Hailey, *Native Administration*, pp. 388, 389).

23. Government of Great Britain, High Commissioner for Basutoland, the Bechuanaland Protectorate, and Swaziland, *Official Gazette, 1950* (Pretoria: High Commissioner's Stationery Office, 1951), p. 1. The *Gazette* itself turned out to be an important indicator of administrative activity. During the 1950s, there was an substantial increase in the number of British proclamations designed to meet the demands of the future. Guidelines for the formation of trade unions, for example, were set down in 1951, although the first union was not formed until 1962.

ously resisted subsequent attempts on the part of the British
to diminish their authority by the introduction of new political
frameworks more conducive to the emergence of "modern"
political forces. Proclamations 80 and 81 of 1950 also had the
net effect of enhancing the power of the monarchy by returning to it certain areas of criminal jurisdiction, by allowing for
the setting up of Swazi courts, and by establishing a Swazi National Treasury to be financed by court fines, fees, and head
taxes.[24]

Although the proclamations of 1950 were hardly revolutionary, they had a profound influence on the course of political development in Swaziland, for they gave the Swazi hierarchy a firm base from which to resist subsequent attempts to
diminish its power and, later, from which to launch a concerted bid for political hegemony. Looking back, one can say
that these measures signaled an ebbing of British control over
the course of political developments in Swaziland. While it is
true that the Swazis remained quiescent for a decade and this
loss of control went largely unrecognized by the British, nevertheless, with changed political configurations elsewhere in
Africa, time would be speeded up by events. With the advent
of independence in many African states after 1960, the implementation of apartheid in South Africa and South Africa's interest in Swaziland as a possible Bantustan, and the importation of such concepts as Pan-Africanism, the British attempted
to move the Swazis toward a nonracial one-man, one-vote constitution. At that point, the Swazi traditionalists as well as the
REAC turned increasingly recalcitrant. Because of the decisions of the 1950s, each group would have a firm base from
which to operate. This meant that not only would it prove
difficult to override their wishes, but also, when new forces
hostile to both the REAC and the ngwenyama sprang up,
there would be no official channel for their political activities.
With the benefit of hindsight, therefore, it seems surprising
that the British authorities did not realize the potential implications of their actions; for much of the bitterness that accompanied the decolonization process stemmed from an under-
estimation of the very forces the administration had, in fact,

24. Doxey, *The High Commission Territories*, p. 24.

strengthened. In short, the two-block political arrangement created by administrative activity in the 1940s and 1950s made any movement toward new political arrangements difficult unless both groups agreed to these new directions and saw in them an opportunity for the enhancement of their power.[25] As long as they regarded any change in the status quo as detrimental to their position, they would resist. Perhaps these difficulties could have been avoided had the British moved quickly toward the creation of a single territory-wide legislature. When they did not do so for over a decade, positions hardened to such an extent that it was the form of the political system, not the ultimate goal of independence or even the pace of its attainment, that was to dominate the political life of Swaziland from 1960 until 1966. It is to these antic events that the remainder of this work is devoted.

1960, A Watershed Year

Before attempting to unravel the complicated political developments of the 1960s, however, I shall pause to give the reader a generalized portrait of Swaziland in 1960. This is an excellent point at which to view the cumulative effect that the economic and political changes outlined above had had on life in Swaziland, for January 1960 is an important watershed. At that time, there were no political parties, no trade unions, no territorial legislature, and no general participation in the politics of the area. Within a few short years, all of these came into being, and the quest for a viable political framework overshadowed all other problems, even that of economic development. In 1960 a number of studies were either conducted or released, studies that indicated the extent to which demographic, social, and economic changes had already occurred and the probable lines of future development.[26] Taken to-

25. The REAC, for example, seems to have received its re-creation as a mandate to play a greater, not a lessened, role in the affairs of the Swazis.

26. See especially J. F. Holleman (ed.), *Experiment in Swaziland* (Durban: University of Natal Press, 1964); Daniel, *Geography of the Rural Economy of Swaziland;* T. J. D. Fair and L. P. Green, "Preparing for Swaziland's Future Economic Growth," *Optima* 10, no. 4 (December 1960): 194–206; idem *Development in Africa* (Johannesburg: University of Witwatersrand Press, 1962); Government of Great Britain, *Basutoland, Be-*

gether, they illustrate the extent to which Swaziland had changed since the time of the Kuper and Marwick studies outlined in chapter one, and also the ways in which Swaziland had changed hardly at all.

What emerges is a portrait of substantial but not overwhelming change, of a society collectively in transition but with important, even vital, sectors, both economical and political, under traditional control. For example, 38 percent of the Europeans and 34 percent of the Eurafricans were urbanized, but only 7 to 8 percent of the Swazis.[27] Yet increasing migration to the cities by the Swazis had begun, and their level of urbanization would nearly double within the next five years. It was these urban Swazis for the most part who would form the bulk of support for the new political parties and who would offer a concerted challenge to the Europeans and to the traditionalists.

Economically, the development of the major plantations and their subsidiary industries had created a groundswell that markedly increased per capita income and drew substantial numbers of Swazis into the cash sector of the economy. It is estimated that between 72 percent and 88 percent of all households in Swaziland received some cash income in 1960, although a much smaller percentage was able to live purely on their cash incomes.[28] Overall, economic advances had been greater among Europeans and had been confined to a relatively small number of geographical areas, the Piggs Peak–Havelock complex, the Mbabane-Usutu-Manzini matrix, and the Big Bend and Tshaneni-Mhlume area. There were thus two major gaps that were to have an important impact on the politics of decolonization. The first was between the Europeans as a group and the Swazis. The second was between urban and rural dwellers regardless of race. For example, it would be those Europeans living in the area south of the Usutu Valley who had not shared very substantially in the

chuanaland Protectorate, and Swaziland: Report of an Economic Survey Mission; and Government of Swaziland, Census of Swaziland, 1956 (Mbabane: Government Printer, 1958).

27. Holleman, Experiment in Swaziland, p. 325.

28. Ibid., pp. 255–274.

economic gains of the past decade who would eventually call for South Africa to "buy them out" and make of Swaziland a Bantustan. Furthermore, those Swazis who became urbanized, while increasing their total incomes vis-à-vis their rural counterparts, would most vigorously protest the privileged position of the Europeans.

Along with increasing rates of urbanization and per capita income, 1960 was also a watershed year in terms of international influences. Increasing numbers of refugees were entering the country from South Africa following the massacre at Sharpeville in March and the subsequent banning of the Pan-African and African National congresses. Later, with the outbreak of fighting in Mozambique, refugees came also from the Portuguese-controlled areas. Swaziland's long, open, unprotected borders with South Africa and Mozambique, as well as British reluctance to turn away political refugees, meant that Swaziland was attracting increasing numbers of refugees. They usually brought with them political ideas and often participated in the politics of Swaziland, giving support to those political parties that developed in opposition to the Swazi traditionalists and Europeans. They also prompted attempts, some legal, some extralegal, on the part of the South Africans and Portuguese to recapture them. Furthermore, their activities, real or imagined, strained the already overburdened national police of Swaziland, who were increasingly hard pressed to cope with rising urbanization, European immigration, and juvenile crime.[29]

Yet for all the ferment and change associated with 1960, it would be easy to overestimate the scope of change. As late as 1966 fully 87 percent of the Swazis remained more or less encapsulated in their rural, traditional setting and were only marginally affected by the changes outlined above, particularly with regard to politics. There can be little question that the forces we have labeled "modern" did set in motion developments that seemed conducive to the passing of the old order, and the new politicians who would arise in the 1960s seemed to have the weight of history on their side, particularly in view

29. Government of Swaziland, *Annual Report of the Commissioner of Police* (Mbabane: Government Printer, 1959, 1960, 1961, 1962).

of events elsewhere in Africa. Yet, as the remainder of this study will show, it was the extent to which the traditional Swazi political system remained intact that would ultimately determine the political future of Swaziland. At the same time, the transitional nature of the 1960s suggested to many observers—Swazi, European settler, and British—that the forces of change would lead to a breakup of the Swazi traditional hierarchy. These miscalculations concerning the political efficacy of the new forces, more than any other single factor, thrust the ngwenyama into the maelstrom of modern politics, caused the Europeans to overplay their hand, and ultimately caused the defeat of the very forces that seemed headed for triumph.

3

The Beginnings of Modern Politics

IN A SPEECH TO THE SOUTH AFRICAN PARLIAMENT ON
February 3, 1960, British Prime Minister Harold Macmillan
used his now famous "wind of change" phrase to symbolize the
forces propelling the African territories toward independence
and the new political configurations that would accompany
decolonization. In many ways, Macmillan's trip to Southern
Africa heralded a new era in Swaziland, one characterized by
the beginnings of "modern" politics and a search for a national, integrative political framework.[1]

The members of the Reconstituted European Advisory Council responded to the quickening pace of political life by presenting a memorandum to the secretary of state requesting that
the British government establish a multiracial legislative council in Swaziland in which the Swazi traditionalists and European settlers would share power on an equal basis. Speaking
for Her Majesty's government, the British high commissioner
for Basutoland, Bechuanaland, and Swaziland, Sir John P.
Maud, promised that the matter would be taken under advise-
ment. Little was done until April 1960, when the ngwenyama,

1. In this context, I am using the term "modern" to denote the new
techniques associated with formal mass participation in politics, including political parties, political competition by organized associational
groups, and participation in nationwide elections. In the following chapters, I shall often refer to the new political leaders as "detribalized." This
is taken to mean individuals who have been absorbed into the cash sector
of the economy, who have participated in one or more associational groups,
and who have lost their allegiance to the local tribal authorities.

Sobhuza II, proposed that the Swazi National Council and the REAC abandon their previous advisory role and meet together as a legislative council (although the ngwenyama was careful to stipulate that the new legislative council was to have no jurisdiction over Swazi law and custom or over the existing Swazi mineral and land holdings). This sharing of power between European and Swazi traditionalists was designed to lead to a type of race federation, with both groups cognizant of the differences between their respective constituencies.

Subsequently, many Swazi leaders were to claim that the ngwenyama never meant an actual fifty-fifty sharing of power and that this offer was just a plot to ensure European support of the monarchy. Be that as it may, Sobhuza II did express a desire for a sharing of power and proposed that "the European public should elect representatives according to its established system of elections and that the Swazis should select theirs in the manner which was most familiar and suitable to the Swazi people." [2] Since this process would mean that the Swazi representatives would be chosen by the traditional *tinkhundla* method and would have severely limited the political role of the emerging urbanized Swazi elite, the British administration was cool to the proposals. Having gone through the process of constitutional reform in a number of African countries, the British Colonial Office seemed reluctant to sanction a constitutional arrangement that would, it felt, be subsequently replaced with a one-man, one-vote system.

Resident Commissioner Brian (later Sir Brian) Marwick also opposed the European and Swazi proposals on the grounds that the modern political forces would be excluded. Brian Marwick was extremely knowledgeable concerning the affairs of Swaziland. He was a recognized authority on Swazi law and custom and spoke siSwati fluently. He had previously served in Swaziland in 1925 and in Nigeria between 1937 and 1941, returning to Swaziland in 1942 where he acted as district officer and first assistant secretary.

Following an absence from the territory from 1949 until 1956, he was appointed resident commissioner. Marwick thus

2. Government of Great Britain, Colonial Office, *Swaziland, 1960* (London: Her Majesty's Stationery Office, 1961), p. 3.

brought wide experience and expertise to the situation as well as a vision for the future of Swaziland, a government for Swaziland elected under a nonracial one-man, one-vote constitution. This was, of course, a view of the future that clashed directly with that held by most Europeans and the Swazi traditional hierarchy, for neither of these groups wished to risk losing their political power to the emerging counterelites who advocated modern political techniques.

Responding to the British suggestion that a more democratic form of representation be developed, the ngwenyama publicly expressed opposition to the constitutional forms elsewhere in Africa and made a definite, if somewhat dubious, connection between the British constitutional suggestions and the difficulties in other African states:

> the principle of "one man, one vote" was totally unfamiliar to the Africans and there was no good reason why such practices should be forced on the latter. . . . The policy of "one man, one vote" was fatal for Africa because the race with the largest numbers would swallow the other race; take away their rights and nationalize their institutions. The prospect of this brought about that fear which was at the root of all the troubles in Africa.[3]

Any cooperation, the ngwenyama stated, would have to take place within a framework that recognized the existing primacy of the two European and traditional Swazi groups, the REAC and the Swazi National Council. After reading chapter one, with its portrayal of the present extent of the ngwenyama's

3. Quoted in the *Times of Swaziland* (Mbabane) 58, no. 27 (July 1, 1960): 1. The *Times*, which first appeared in 1896, had been little more than a social sheet devoted to the coverage of teas and sporting events until Mr. William Talbot assumed the editorship in 1960. During the next seven years, the *Times* became an important forum for political opinion. As Swaziland's only paper, it served an important function in providing the various political groups access to the literate public. There were, of course, South African papers available in Swaziland during this period; but only the *Times* faithfully published the speeches, manifestos, and programs of all the political parties. Because it carefully recorded the political ephemera and documented the rise and fall of so many of the parties in the 1960s, the *Times* became a far more important repository for political data than the average weekly newspaper. Since the demise of the various political parties, it remains the only source of some materials.

sweeping power, the reader may well find it difficult to under-
stand the ngwenyama's cautious attitude, his concern over the
emergence of new political leaders, and his fear of a one-man,
one-vote arrangement.

It should be born in mind that during the early 1960s,
Sobhuza II was by no means fully aware of his potential political power; and he, along with most of the tribal hierarchy, had
no realistic basis on which to judge their power vis-à-vis the
new forces. Furthermore, his European advisers did much to
play on this basic fear and were quick to point out the fate of
many African traditional authorities during their respective
decolonization experiences. Certainly, on balance, independence had generally meant a reduced political role for these
authorities. In terms of Swaziland, therefore, the post-1960
period may conveniently be divided into two periods.

The first, running from 1960 until late 1965, was a period
of challenges to the traditional hierarchy, first by British designs for the new constitution, then by the newly emergent
Pan-African oriented political parties, and finally by the European settlers within Swaziland. During this period, it was by
no means certain that the forces led by the ngwenyama would
triumph. It was only after 1965 that the magnitude of success
achieved by the traditional authorities became apparent, and
that Sobhuza II emerged as the political prime mover of
Swaziland.

Reaction to the ngwenyama's 1960 proposals was not long
in coming. The Nationalist government of South Africa welcomed his "realistic statements"; the European in the territory
generally applauded his "good sense and moderation"; and
the modern, detribalized Swazis and non-Swazi Africans expressed surprise that there was to be no independent political
role for them under the proposed constitution.[4] The British
authorities maintained their official silence, but it became
widely known that they did not favor the proposals of the
REAC or the ngwenyama. From the time of Macmillan's

4. Assuming themselves to be left out of any sharing of political power,
these modern elements then set about forming a series of political parties.
They might have done so in any case, but the ngwenyama's views on the
proposed legislative council clearly hastened the process.

speech onward, the ngwenyama and his closest advisers in the Swazi National Council moved to limit their dependence on the British (to whom they had traditionally looked to stem South African influence) and gravitated toward closer cooperation with the Europeans in Swaziland and with elements in South Africa. This did not mean, as was widely alleged, that the ngwenyama favored apartheid or that he wished to see Swaziland become a Bantustan. It did mean that Sobhuza II feared for his political position and was willing to take help from almost any source in order to maintain himself. At this point, he simply sought allies to prevent the British from imposing a constitution that would reduce his power and would encourage the detribalized Swazi to seek alternatives to the tribal framework.

This latter group was already moving in that direction, for during July 1960 they formed Swaziland's first political party— led by Mr. John June Nquku, a Zulu originally from South Africa—which signaled a new era in the life of the territory. The Swaziland Progressive party (SPP) was an outgrowth of the old Swaziland Progressive Association, a cultural organization for the Swazi intelligentsia formed in 1928. Mr. Nquku was born in Pietermaritzburg in 1899 and was educated at St. Chad's College in Natal. On his arrival in Swaziland, he became a principal in and then an inspector of African schools in the territory.

He wrote several pamphlets, including a geography of Swaziland, a praiseful account of Sobhuza II's reign entitled *Bayete,* and a series of Swazi folk tales, *Amaqhawe AkwaNgwane.*[5] After resigning from the educational administration in 1940, he became a member of the Swazi National Council. In 1944, when five splinter Zionist churches formed the United Christian Church of Africa, he became secretary-general of the new organization and, in the following year, was chosen president of the Swaziland Progressive Association and editor of *Ngwane,* its newspaper. Serving as president from 1945 until 1960 gave Nquku the opportunity to become widely known, and he had been preparing for his entrance into politics for some time.

5. For example, J. J. Nquku, *Geography of Swaziland* (Bremersdorp, Swaziland: Servite Fathers, 1936), is still available in English.

His choice of avenues, particularly the creation of a new party, had been stimulated by the May 6, 1960, visit of Aloysius K. Barden, director of Ghana's Bureau of African Affairs.[6] The SPP soon attracted a number of urbanized Swazis, including Dr. Ambrose Phesheya Zwane, the first Swazi physician. Dr. Zwane was born in 1922 in Manzini, Swaziland, and was educated at Fort Hare and the University of Witwatersrand, South Africa; he was attracted to the African National Congress of South Africa during the 1950s. He resigned his medical post with the Swaziland government in March 1960 and joined the Swaziland Progressive party, soon becoming its secretary-general.

The Swaziland Progressive party inherited the general principles of the old Swaziland Progressive Association and supported "the essential dignity of every human being irrespective of Race, Color or Creed, to see that every human being regardless of Race, Color or Creed is given freedom of worship, expression, movement, assembly and association." [7] It also stood for a nonracial constitutional monarchy, with universal suffrage and the principle of one man, one vote. Initially, the SPP attracted a number of urbanized Swazis and non-Swazi Africans who did not feel a part of the Swazi traditional structure and who might well have formed the basis for an emergent national movement. At the same time, from its inception the party suffered from a number of weaknesses. As a Zulu, Nquku was suspect in the eyes of many Swazis, and his personal style of leadership irritated others within the party to the extent that it was constantly wracked by personal, financial, and ideological disputes that hampered its effectiveness. Also, perhaps because of its Ghanaian connections, the party leaders

6. Barden had not been well received in Swaziland during his trip to South Africa, and little was made of his visit by the British or the Swazi traditionalists. Nquku, however, welcomed him warmly; and Nquku's professed belief in progressive political ideas and Pan-Africanism found a sympathetic ear and eventually financial support, which came from Ghana to the Progressive party (Stevens, *Lesotho, Botswana, and Swaziland,* p. 203). For a detailed examination of the workings of the African bureau and Ghana's foreign policy during this period, see W. Scott Thompson, *Ghana's Foreign Policy, 1957–1966* (Princeton: Princeton University Press, 1969).

7. Swaziland Progressive Association, "Constitution of the Swaziland Progressive Constitution" (mimeographed, Mbabane, 1929), p. 1.

became overly concerned with Pan-Africanism and the rhetoric of African socialism and generally ignored the need for grass-roots organization in the countryside.

With the formation of the SPP and the continuing demands for a territory-wide legislative council, the British government began moving toward the creation of a constitutional committee. As the process of constitutional advance was already under way in Basutoland and the Bechuanaland Protectorate, it became increasingly important that some type of arrangement be worked out for Swaziland. The form of that arrangement was of particular importance to the British; for Swaziland, with its large number of European settlers, could, if properly developed, serve as a nonracial challenge to the South African form of racial apartheid.[8] Constitutional talks began in November 1960, and the British administration invited a number of delegates, most of whom were regarded as important figures in their respective communities. Representing the Swazis were Prince Makhosini, Prince Lutho, P. L. Dlamini, S. T. M. Sukati, J. S. Matsebula, A. K. Hlope, D. Lukhele, J. J. Nquku, Dr. A. Zwane, and Obed Mabuza, and for the Europeans, A. Millin, H. Pierce, C. F. Todd, R. P. Stephens, H. D. G. Fitzpatrick, B. P. Stewart, G. Bordihn, C. S. Hubbard, Willie Meyer, Eric Winn, Dr. David Hynd, and E. Bowman. The Eurafrican community of over 2,000 persons was not represented at these early talks.

Brian Marwick, who presided over the meetings, was unable to get anything like a consensus on the form the proposed constitution should take. The committee itself seemed uninterested in finding a compromise framework. Instead, it broke down into factions from the very beginning with the progressives such as Nquku and Zwane using the meetings as a politi-

8. This concern became increasingly acute after the South African decision to become a republic and to withdraw from the Commonwealth. See, for example, the British Information Service, *Apartheid: Challenge to British Policy* (London: Her Majesty's Stationery Office, 1964). Sir John Maud, high commissioner to Basutoland, Swaziland, and the Bechuanaland Protectorate, clearly had in mind the creation of a multiracial state in Swaziland that would stand as a counterpoint to South Africa and directly influenced Brian Marwick in this regard. See especially his "Challenge of the High Commission Territories," *African Affairs* 63 (April 1964): 94–103; and "My Hopes for Swaziland," *Swaziland Recorder*, no. 10 (March–June 1963): 11–13.

cal forum, while the conservative Europeans and the Swazis used them to try to maintain their existing preeminence. Neither group seriously considered an alternative to their original proposals. The meetings of the committee took place against the backdrop of the socioeconomic changes outlined in chapter two, and it seemed clear to the participants that Swaziland was about to undergo a period of political transition as well. What was less clear to them was the direction of that change. The Europeans in particular felt that they could hold on to a great deal of political power simply by biding their time. As unrealistic as this view turned out to be, at the moment it seemed to be a distinct possibility, considering the adamant stand of the Swazi National Council, which insisted that, whatever the dimensions of political change, the traditional authorities not be undercut.[9]

In this context, then, it was upsetting for many Europeans and Swazi traditionalists to hear the Progressive party talking about one man, one vote and rejecting a multiracial government with reserved seats for Europeans. Many were quick to blame "Communists" and "refugees" from South Africa and to write the Progressive party off as "dangerously radical." [10] The representatives of this constituency on the constitutional committee simply refused to consider the proposals of the Swaziland Progressive party and reiterated their previous position that political power in Swaziland must be shared by Europeans and the Swazi traditional hierarchy by means of a dual electoral roll and a weighted assembly providing each group with half the representatives. Faced with this hostile attitude and badly outnumbered on the committee itself, the leaders of the Swaziland Progressive party decided to take the issue to the general public and made a number of strong statements:

9. It should be remembered that a contemporary debate was swirling around the issue of whether or not Africans should even be allowed access to distilled liquor. The *Times of Swaziland,* for example, was attacked for advocating even limited access: "If the African is to be permitted free access to liquor surely it would be better that he should learn the niceties of drinking in his own properly equipped bars under the supervision of firm and competent African bartenders" (*Times of Swaziland* 58, no. 52 [December 23, 1960]: 1).

10. European Advisory Council, "Minutes of the Reconstituted Advisory Council, 1961" (mimeographed by the government secretary, Mbabane, 1962), p. 15; and the *Times of Swaziland* 59, no. 8 (February 24, 1961): 4.

Indeed the old political trick of fooling the Swaziland public is still being carried dangerously too far. It ought to be halted or stopped lest it drags the country to a dangerous situation and adds further fuel to the already deteriorating race relations. It is lulling all Swazilanders into complacency at a moment when they ought to be wide awake to meet the most dangerous challenge of their lives. Their fate and that of their country is being decided *in camera* and behind tightly bolted doors. The dictatorship of the past must be fought to the bitter end in order that the public may be freed from fear of reprisals.[11]

Opposition to Nquku grew within the committee, and he was expelled on May 18, 1961, for his "disruptive" tactics. When a majority of the committee then recommended that the ngwenyama be given the right to pass judgment on any political party and to ban their participation in the political life of the country, Dr. Zwane and Obed Mpangele Mabuza resigned from the committee, citing this "violation of the freedom of political organization" and the "unreasonable" expulsion of the SPP president.[12]

There can be little doubt that the decision to leave the committee and to adopt an increasingly uncompromising stance was influenced by Nquku's and Zwane's perceptions of what had happened elsewhere in Africa, particularly in the Gold Coast. As they saw it, Kwame Nkrumah had refused to accept the conservative findings of the various constitutional commissions and, by developing a call for "Independence Now," had provoked a wave of mass support. As with the Conventions People's party, the SPP hoped to circumvent the existing power elite by appealing directly to the masses and to emerge victorious. The attempt to emulate this tactic overlooked the differences in the political situations, especially the strength of the traditional authorities and the small number of Swazi who, under any circumstances, would be willing to break with their king. This oversight was to greatly hamper the SPP's drive for power and was further compounded by the failure of the SPP leadership to organize effective local branches and transform the party into a true mass organization.

11. *Times of Swaziland* 59, no. 18 (May 5, 1961): 5.
12. D. V. Cowen, *Report on Constitutional Reform* (Cape Town: Lincey and Watson, 1961), p. 9. See also Cowen's *The Foundations of Freedom* (Cape Town and New York: Oxford University Press, 1961).

Nevertheless, during the spring of 1961, the SPP made a real effort to press for a solution to Swaziland's political problems. Its leaders called on Professor D. V. Cowen, professor of comparative law at the University of Cape Town, to draw up a constitution that would take into account the existing political situation, but with an eye toward future constitutional development. Cowen was a distinguished authority on constitutional law and had been associated with the drawing up of several constitutions in Basutoland from the mid-1950s onward. His report, when finally released, was seminal and served as the basis for the political platforms of a number of parties; it greatly influenced the course of constitutional development in Swaziland. At the same time, while Cowen arrived in June, his report was not published until late September 1961; and the impetus that the SPP should have gained from the report was largely undercut by a number of intervening developments. On one hand, Nquku and Zwane became embroiled in a series of public attacks on each other, thereby discrediting the party as a whole. Furthermore, much public attention was shifted from the political sphere with the announcement by the British government in August 1961 that Swaziland was to have a territory-wide railroad. Finally, the racial segregation issue on which the Cowen report placed particular emphasis was greatly blunted by the contemporary recommendations of the constitutional committee that antidiscrimination legislation be passed at once.

To take each of these developments in turn, during July 1961, while J. J. Nquku was outside Swaziland on a fund-raising tour, Dr. Zwane led the executive committee of the party in expelling Mr. Nquku for "alleged misappropriation of party funds" and "bigmanism." [13] On hearing the news, Mr. Nquku quickly rushed back to Mbabane, regrouped his forces, and expelled Zwane for making "unauthorized statements." In the face of this action, the executive committee wavered and accepted Nquku's account of the funds. Zwane was forced to recant and subsequently rejoined the party. The incident convinced him, however, that the road to power within the SPP

13. On July 6, 1961, he returned from Ghana. *Rand Daily Mail* (Johannesburg), July 7, 1961, p. 11.

did not lie through the executive apparatus, which was staffed with Nquku's cronies, but through the creation of a youth wing which he, Zwane, could use as a base of support.

The subsequent establishment of a youth wing further exacerbated the differences between Nquku and Zwane. On February 4, 1962, while Nquku was in Johannesburg on his way to London, eight Swazi youths accosted him and tried to grab his passport. The incident apparently grew out of the number of scholarships that the government of Ghana had awarded to the Swaziland Progressive party for disbursement. Nquku assigned them but insisted that the students sign a statement of allegiance to him, renouncing Zwane and Dumisa Dlamini, the head of the youth league.[14] When they refused, Nquku kept the scholarships and the airline tickets to Accra. Confronted by the students, he had them taken into custody by the South African police and sent back to Swaziland while he flew to London.

Back in Swaziland, Zwane used the incident to move against Nquku again. This time he accused Nquku of failing to display loyalty to the ngwenyama and of working for a constitutional arrangement that would leave Sobhuza powerless. Of course, this was largely a smoke-screen issue, for when Zwane eventually formed a second branch of the SPP (renaming it in April 1963 the Ngwane National Liberatory Congress [NNLC]), he espoused the same position. Once again, the executive committee of the SPP refused to substitute Zwane for Nquku; and Benjamin Simelane, acting president of the SPP, supported by Mrs. R. D. Twala and O. B. Mabuza, expelled Zwane. This time Zwane refused to recant, and on February 14 he called a general meeting of the party at Kwaluseni, near Matsapa. At the meeting he introduced resolutions calling on Nquku to return to Swaziland and formally disassociating the SPP from Nquku's statements. While it is not clear exactly how many persons were at the meeting or how many actually voted for the resolutions, Zwane claimed that they constituted a majority of the membership, and he went off to head a new SPP with Dumisa Dlamini as secretary-general.

Despite his air of insouciance, Nquku was badly hurt politi-

14. *Times of Swaziland* 60, no. 6 (February 9, 1962): 6.

cally. Although the rump version of the SPP, which kept the official name for itself, contested the Zwane faction for over a year, the split eventually cost Nquku valuable and much needed support, able leadership, and Dumisa Dlamini, perhaps the most effective political activist in the party. Clement Dumisa Dlamini was a nephew of the ngwenyama. After studying briefly at Pius XII University College at Roma, Basutoland (now the University of Botswana, Lesotho, and Swaziland), he returned to Swaziland in 1960.[15] He soon joined the SPP and became head of the youth league. His dynamic personality and impressive oratorical skill made him an important political figure. Although his political career was to be marred by a number of criminal charges and some erratic behavior, he, more than anyone else on the political scene, was able to galvanize the actions of large numbers of persons during the civil disorders of May and June 1963. He soon emerged as a force to be reckoned with.

Nquku's troubles were not over with the defection of Dumisa and Dr. Zwane. A number of misfortunes occurred in rapid succession. During February 1962, a fire of suspicious origin destroyed his car; and in June, while he was in Egypt, another fire destroyed three rooms of his home and most of the SPP records. Finally, in August 1962 O. M. Mabuza, new secretary-general of the Nquku wing of the SPP, sought a court injunction blocking Nquku's bank account; and together with B. M. Simelane and K. T. Samketi, they formed yet another "purified" version of the SPP which "suspended" Nquku. Nquku, off in Europe, refused to acknowledge the suspension and indicated that the entire affair was "nothing but fabrication concocted by some power seekers in the party." [16] When Nquku failed to acknowledge the authority of the new executive, Mr. Samketi turned to the Zwane wing and held a joint meeting with Zwane's aides while he was out of the country. When Zwane returned, he too refused to accept the authority of the new group and was "expelled" by Simelane and Samketi. This

15. For a brief description of the university, see R. P. Stevens, "Southern Africa's Multiracial University," *African Report* 9, no. 3 (March 1964): 16–18.

16. *Times of Swaziland* 60, no. 3 (August 17, 1962): 5.

expulsion had little effect on Zwane's improving political fortunes; for on his way back to Swaziland, he and Dumisa Dlamini had been detained by the South African special branch and held at Grey's police station near Johannesburg. Although they were both soon released, the incident earned them widespread support in Swaziland. Finally, on September 30 Samketi called for a general meeting of all members of all three branches of the SPP. When only thirty persons, many of whom had simply wandered in off the streets, bothered to attend, Samketi and Simelane dismissed the group and promised that a special conference would be called soon. None was ever forthcoming. Eventually Simelane drifted back to Nquku's group, and the third splinter of the SPP was taken over by Mr. Mabuza. By the year's end, only the Zwane wing of the party remained politically credible.

Obviously, many of the incidents cited above occurred after the publication of the Cowen report. But the tone of political action had been set, and Nquku became widely regarded as a Falstaffian figure, not to be taken seriously. Actually, of course, he could look back on subsequent events with some personal vindication, for his ideas of a nonracial constitution with one man, one vote were eventually adopted. In the meantime, he contented himself with enjoying the financial rewards and prestige accruing to the president of a political party.[17] The negative impact of his actions on the nationalist movement, however, was considerable.

If the leadership struggles were not enough to undercut the impact of the SPP's constitutional proposals, there was in addition the announcement of the beginnings of the Swaziland railroad which caused great excitement throughout the territory. During August 1961, agreement was reached between Great Britain, Swaziland, Portugal, the Anglo-American Corporation (parent company of the newly formed Swaziland Iron Ore Development Company), and the Colonial Development Corporation to build the railroad to the border of Mozam-

17. His travels were considerable and he was forever appearing at the United Nations or in London or Accra as a leader of the "people's struggle." As late as 1965, for example, he was invited to the Tri-Continental Conference in Havana as a "freedom fighter," despite the fact that his party had essentially dwindled down to himself and A. W. N. Nxumalo.

bique where it would be connected to the existing line from Goba, Mozambique, to the port of Lourenço Marques. In exchange for its contribution to the building of the railroad, Swaziland Iron Ore Development Company received the exclusive right to a twenty-one-year lease over 1,052 acres with a further guarantee of renewal.[18] Anglo-American had secured long-term contracts for the iron ore from two Japanese firms, the Yamata Iron and Steel Company and the Fuji Iron and Steel Company. These contracts called for the delivery of twelve million tons of ore over a ten-year period. The huge financial empire of Sir Ernest Oppenheimer had been expanded by his son, Harry Oppenheimer, and by 1962, the Anglo-American Corporation stood at the head of a large number of companies such as DeBeers Consolidated Mines, Anglo-American Investment Trust, West Rand Investment Trust, Orange Free State Investment Trust, Vereeniging Estates, Anglo-American Industrial Corporation, Rand Selection Corporation, Charter Consolidated, Anglo-American Corporation of Canada, Zambian Anglo-American, Anglo-American Corporation of Rhodesia, and Boart and Hard Metals Products. With over $1.5 billion in direct assets and control over nearly $2 billion more, such a corporation, it was felt, could well provide the leadership in developing the private sector of the economy in Swaziland. At least this was the view taken by many in the territory, and the resulting enthusiasm for the future of the country, at least briefly, eclipsed the constitutional concerns and undercut some of the SPP's more dire pronouncements.[19]

18. Anglo-American Corporation, press release, June 13, 1962, p. 1.

19. Those readers interested in the flood of articles devoted to the railroad should consult N. Herd, "Green Light on the Swaziland Railroad," *Industrial Review of Africa* 12, no. 10 (May 1961): 8; L. A. W. Hawkins, "Excellent Progress with Railway," *Swaziland Recorder*, no. 13 (January–March 1964): 9–13; idem, "Important Ore Line Will Be Ready for Traffic," *Railway Engineering* 8 (1964): 26–27; idem, "Rich Iron Ore Deposits Give Swaziland Its Long-Awaited Railroad," *Optima* 14, no. 2, (June 1964): 84–87; idem, "Swaziland and Its Ocean Outlet," *African Roads* 21, no. 4 (April 1964): 12–13; Norman Herd, "Track Beds Being Prepared," *Swaziland Recorder*, no. 12 (September–December 1963): 23–25; C. M. Kruger, "Contract to Supply Rails," *Swaziland Recorder*, no. 6 (March–June 1962): 27; T. E. Reilly, "Swaziland's Mine Railway Project," *South African Mining Engineering Journal* 72 (September 1961): 685–687;

A third factor that tended to reduce the impact of the Cowen report was the action of the constitutional committee in combating discrimination in the territory. In this area, the British government and the Swazi leaders were in complete agreement; and whatever they might have felt privately, the European members of the committee accepted the need to come to an accommodation with the Swazi traditionalists on this issue. On June 12, the working committee of the constitutional committee reached an agreement that called for the elimination of racial discrimination under the law. This was eventually accepted by the entire constitutional committee and subsequently by the REAC. In an attempt to lend stature to the committee's report, the British Foreign Office sent Sir Charles Arden-Clarke to Swaziland. He too pledged his support for a multiracial solution that would eliminate racial discrimination in the territory.[20] Although the official government proclamation was not issued until October 24, 1961, and not implemented until the following March, the adoption of the resolution by the constitutional committee was widely regarded as a significant step forward for the social harmony of the country and an important political milestone. The Anti-Discrimination Proclamation of 1961 outlawed segregation and segregated facilities in banks, cinemas, hotels, theaters, bars, and dining rooms and made invalid section 19 of the Immorality Ordinance of 1903 which forbade sexual relations between European women and African men.

The political importance of these measures should not be underestimated. Although racial discrimination undoubtedly remained, the law was now on the side of its elimination. There were, hence, few concrete statutes that the emerging Swazi politicians could attack directly, and they were forced to adopt increasingly abstract and vague positions in the area of social action in order to try to gain popular support. Only in the economic field were these grievances so blatant and widespread that they could be turned into political activity.

D. Smith, "Railroad Key to Many New Industries," *Swaziland Recorder*, no. 16 (September–December 1964): 15–19; and G. M. Thain "Swaziland Railroad," *Swaziland Recorder*, no. 2 (March–June 1961): 13.

20. *Johannesburg Star* (Johannesburg), September 16, 1961, p. 1.

The passage of the antidiscrimination measures undercut the appeal of the parties, because in the minds of many it indicated that the Swazi traditionalists had been able to accomplish these improvements precisely because they had been able to work with the Europeans. For their part, the Europeans' realpolitik on the issue of segregation by law opened the way for a continued alliance with the traditionalists and effectively shut off, for the time being at least, the possibility of an anti-European political alliance between the newly emerging politicians and the traditional hierarchy.

For all these reasons, then, the publication of the Cowen report did not generate much political impetus for the SPP. Yet the report itself was of considerable importance for the political future of Swaziland. Eventually it was to serve as the basis of the party platform not only for the SPP but for the Ngwane National Liberatory Congress, the Joint Council of Swaziland Political Parties, the Swaziland Democratic party, and the National Convention party; and ultimately, it would form the basis of the Swaziland constitution of 1967. At the time of its release to the general public, however, the Cowen report was not widely acclaimed. In the first place, it came out squarely against a proposed division of power between the Swazis and the Europeans: "It is unhealthy, racial-communal representation being a canker in the body politic, which will perpetuate racial thinking in Swaziland and do harm in souring race relations. It would give the whites at one jump, an enormous ascension of political power, coupled with their already overwhelming economic power." [21] The report also stressed the need for democratic elections and the spuriousness of many of the claims against such elections: "In this regard the Progressive Party is particularly disquieted by King Sobhuza's public pronouncements that he is opposed to the existence of political parties among the Swazi and does not believe that modern forms of democratic government can be successfully worked out in African countries." [22] Cowen stressed the fact that, while the ultimate goal of the SPP was a political system based on the one-man, one-vote principle, he recognized that there would have to be a number of interim steps toward

21. Cowen, *Report on Constitutional Reform*, p. 17.   22. *Ibid.*, p. 17.

that end. He therefore proposed that a legislative council be set up with its membership consisting of ten Swazis nominated by the ngwenyama (whom the report constantly referred to as "the Paramount Chief"), forty-two members elected by universal adult suffrage, five official members drawn from the British administration, and three members nominated by the high commissioner for Basutoland, Bechuanaland, and Swaziland "to represent interests not otherwise represented." [23]

In addition to directly opposing the proposed fifty-fifty sharing of power, the Cowen report also came out against some entrenched prerogatives already enjoyed by the European and Swazi elites. It was especially critical of the tradition that allowed Europeans in Swaziland to vote both in the elections of Swaziland and in those of South Africa. Since 1903, Europeans with British passports had enjoyed what amounted to dual citizenship in both territories. This arrangement had worked fairly well during the relatively quiet 1930s and 1940s; but with the coming to power of the National party in South Africa in 1948, new lines of cleavage developed and many English-speaking Europeans in Swaziland had attempted to limit the growth of the Afrikaans-speaking community of Swaziland. For example, in April 1953 the REAC unanimously passed a resolution urging that British citizenship be a prerequisite for voting in Swaziland. [24]

With decolonization elsewhere in Africa, however, and the increasing opposition to the proposals for a constitution that would limit European power, many Europeans began to look to South Africa for support. This trend, coupled with a dramatic increase in the European population in Swaziland (85 percent from 1946–1956, 50 percent from 1956 to 1961), made the retention of dual voting privileges important to many Europeans. [25] Eventually, Europeans would be faced with just

23. *Ibid.*, p. 20. Cowen clearly had in mind the Eurafrican community, which was likely to go unrepresented in the direct elections.

24. European Advisory Council, "Minutes of the Reconstituted European Advisory Council 1954" (mimeographed by the government secretary, Mbabane, 1954), p. 38.

25. J. E. Spence, "The High Commission Territories with Special Reference to Swaziland," in Burton Benedict (ed.), *Problems of Smaller Territories* (London: Athlone Press, 1967), p. 98.

such a decision and by 1966 would have to choose whether to retain Swazi, British, or South African citizenship; but at this moment in time, the Cowen proposals seemed to be a direct threat to European power in the territory.

The Cowen report also struck hard at the preeminent position of the Swazi traditionalists, particularly the ngwenyama, and called for a marked reduction in the power of the monarchy: "Thus while the Paramount Chief and his Council are likely to continue during the foreseeable future as the repositories of Swazi law and custom and will have an important role to play in government, increasingly this role will be subject to democratic legislative control." [26] Considering that the ngwenyama of Swaziland was a powerful political figure, standing at the head of a centralized monarchy with an effective tribal structure, the Cowen report represented a fundamental challenge to his position. The espousal of the Cowen report by the SPP and subsequently by other parties thrust the monarchy and the politicians into antagonistic camps. Undoubtedly, Cowen and the leadership of the SPP spoke with conviction and concern; but looking back, their espousal of proposals designed to dramatically reduce the power of the ngwenyama severely circumscribed their range of options and cost them an important opportunity to seek a compromise with the forces of the monarchy and thereby undercut the developing alliance with the Europeans. It is quite possible that the political leaders could have reached some basis for cooperation with the ngwenyama, even though they could not have achieved their primary objectives at once. Again one wonders about the extent to which political developments elsewhere in Africa (in the case of Cowen, Basutoland where King Moshoeshoe II was in the process of being eclipsed by the emerging political parties and where essentially different circumstances existed) influenced the course of their thinking and caused them to overestimate their potential political efficacy.[27]

In any case, the Cowen report was not well received in

---

26. Cowen, *Report on Constitutional Reform,* p. 28.

27. For details on the situation in Basutoland, see J. E. Spence, *Lesotho: The Politics of Dependence* (London: Oxford University Press, 1968), pp. 29–54.

Swaziland, and mass support for its findings failed to develop. Even the moderate *Times of Swaziland* found it "fraught with danger for Swaziland." [28] The danger of communal strife, however, lay in ignoring the extent to which the report was valid in its criticisms but invalid in its proposed solutions or, to be more accurate, the way in which these solutions were to be attained. From this point on, all groups in Swaziland suffered increasingly from misconceptions and false impressions and these, more than any single factor, held up the course of constitutional advance for nearly three years.

During December 1961, members of the constitutional committee were invited to London for a round of talks with Secretary of State for Colonies Reginald Maudling. The modern political figures, having removed themselves from the committee, were conspicuous by their absence, and the meetings were dominated by three representatives favoring the status quo, Prince Makhosini, Polycarp Dlamini, and C. F. Todd. All three were to play important roles in the political developments of the next decade. Prince Makhosini was born in 1914 and was educated at Franson Christian Memorial School and the Swazi National School at Matsapa. Originally a teacher, he served as secretary-general and chairman of the Swaziland Teachers' Association and was later appointed to the administration and the Swazi National Council. A staunch conservative and intensely loyal to the ngwenyama, he would eventually be Sobhuza's choice for prime minister. Polycarp Dlamini had had an equally long record of service to the throne, serving as the secretary of the Swazi National Council and national secretary of the Swazi nation. He later became minister for education. C. F. Todd was a South African lawyer who made his home in Swaziland and became a close friend and legal adviser to the ngwenyama. He proved himself to be a skillful politician and was later nominated for the National Assembly by the king's Imbokodvo party. In addition, his many business interests in the territory were not hurt by his association with the ngwenyama.

These initial talks in London were not an outstanding success, since the Swazi and Europeans refused to shift their de-

28. *Times of Swaziland* 59, no. 39 (September 29, 1961): 4.

mands for a fifty-fifty sharing of power and the British moved very slowly to grapple with the seemingly irreconcilable views of these groups and the other political forces in Swaziland. While the deliberations were proceeding, new political forces were appearing in Swaziland. Some Europeans who did not share the majority sentiment of the European community for a fifty-fifty sharing of power, and a number of Africans who opposed the leadership, if not the goals, of the SPP, cast about for a third force, one that would stand between the settler-traditionalists and the increasingly more radical-sounding SPP. One such person was Vincent Rozwadowski. Mr. Rozwadowski had enjoyed a long and varied career. He left Poland during World War II, escaping to Great Britain and then serving with the French underground for the duration of the war. Following its conclusion and his loss of family lands due to the Communist take-over of Poland, he emigrated to South Africa where he became a rancher. Upset over the increasing implementation of apartheid, he and his South African wife moved to Swaziland where they engaged in dairy farming outside of Mbabane. Rozwadowski soon became president of the Swaziland Sebenta Society, a multiracial organization dedicated to the development of a program for adult education among the Swazis. His contacts with such educated Swazis as Simon Nxumalo and Dr. Allen Nxumalo convinced him that there was significant support among the intelligentsia for a moderate political position.

Late in 1961 and early in 1962, Rozwadowski and Simon Nxumalo, together with Jordan Ngubane, a former official of the Liberal party and African National Congress in South Africa, discussed the possibilities of forming a multiracial party, one that would offer a middle-of-the-road alternative to the SPP and the settler-traditionalist alliance. On March 2, 1962, they announced the formation of the Swaziland Democratic party (SDP) to be headed by Simon Nxumalo. Although the son of a chief, Mr. Nxumalo had worked his way from a herd boy and cattle trader to become chairman of the Sebenta Society, where he edited and wrote books for adult education courses and began to take an active interest in the political future of the country.

From its inception, the Democratic party was moderate in both policy and tone. It was manifestly nonracial and enjoyed some liberal European backing. Its platform recognized the need for a king, but wished to make the ngwenyama a constitutional monarch and favored extensive social welfare legislation to improve the living conditions of the average Swazi. It opposed Pan-Africanism as a political philosophy on the grounds that foreign elements, particularly those from Ghana, would intervene in the domestic affairs of Swaziland.[29] The most controversial proposal of the SDP leadership concerned that of suffrage; it favored a qualified franchise although Mr. Nxumalo promised "to work for universal adult suffrage as soon as it is practical." [30]

The SDP spent the next two years raising significant issues and proposing rational, carefully thought-out solutions to them. It dealt with the pressing problems associated with racism, land ownership, constitutional reform, and agricultural development and struck out against all forms of political extremism. For example, its most important pamphlet, *Totalitarianism Opposed,* was a long, closely argued brief against "all forms of totalitarianism such as communism, fascism and apartheid." [31] Yet the party was unable to generate public support for its program. On one hand, its rather modest proposals, however conservative they might now appear, frightened many Europeans and were regarded with suspicion by the Swazi traditional authorities. On the other hand, the SDP was unable to seize the initiative in appealing to the urbanized Swazis who found its program too conservative. It was particularly vulnerable to the Zwane wing of the SPP, against which it was then competing for the allegiance of the urbanized Swazis. The Zwane group gave the appearance of greater organization, power, and oratory which, coupled with substantially more international visibility, made it more impressive.

29. *Ibid.* 60, no. 9 (March 2, 1962): 6.

30. *Ibid.,* no. 10 (March 9, 1962): 7. The SDP leadership's concerns with adult education undoubtedly influenced this choice of franchise qualification. When the proposals did not generate much enthusiasm in Swaziland, the SDP dropped them and espoused the principle of one man, one vote.

31. Swaziland Democratic Party, *Totalitarianism Opposed* (Mbabane: High Commission Printing and Publishing Company, 1962), p. 1.

Then too, the Zwane group was far more willing to capitalize on local grievances and existing frustration with the status quo in order to turn them to political advantage. It therefore seemed to be doing things about problems the SDP leadership were only discussing.

The SDP did make some attempts to challenge the SPP on its own terms. On May 20, 1962, Dr. Zwane addressed an open meeting following his return from Ghana. He had been very impressed by the Ghanian accomplishments and had been well received by the Bureau of African Affairs, which gave him a number of scholarships and provided a small office in Accra that was to serve as a training center for a number of Swazis. Some, including Arthur Khosa, who was to become acting chairman of the Ngwane National Liberatory Congress (NLCC), spent a number of months at the ideological institute in Winneba.[32] At the May meeting, Zwane indicated his growing support for the concepts of Pan-Africanism and African socialism. Simon Nxumalo and a band of SDP stalwarts were present and rose to challenge the assumption that Swaziland should adopt socialism. Dr. Zwane replied, "Because Ghana and other African states were supporting socialism, Swaziland would fall in with them." [33] The heckling continued and the meeting ended in a rather confused fashion. The ideas associated with Pan-Africanism and African solidarity were, however, irrevocably interjected into the political life of Swaziland; and the Zwane group increasingly sought to use their connotations to develop support.

The Zwane faction also began to utilize the growing labor movement in Swaziland for the purpose of political organization. On March 30, 1962, the first trade union in Swaziland, the Swaziland Pulp Timber Workers Union, was formed at Usutu Pulp. Its leaders, H. D. Dlamini and Martin Mdluli, led the first strike on April 4. Although the strike quickly died out, it focused SPP-Zwane attention on the labor movement. Here, economic differentials, paternalistic company attitudes, and other grievances presented a ready set of issues.

32. It now seems clear that Nkrumah did not give unqualified support to the Zwane group but, in fact, hedged his bets by parceling out some support to the Nquku group and eventually to the Imbokodvo National Movement as well.

33. *Times of Swaziland* 60, no. 20 (May 18, 1962): 3.

Dumisa Dlamini in particular was active in the formation of unions at the Havelock Asbestos Mine and Ubombo Ranches and helped to tie the SPP-Zwane group's fortunes to those of the growing labor movement. The other parties were slow to see the possibilities of such action. Belatedly, the SDP did try to organize the workers at the Mhlume Sugar Mill, but for all practical purposes its efforts were eclipsed by the Zwane group. By establishing itself as the most radical party in Swaziland, the Zwane organization had staked out the exciting high ground for itself and was to be the only party that actually gained strength with the passage of time. The other parties invariably began with more support than they were able to sustain.

In addition to the SDP-SPP rivalry, the proliferation of political parties continued throughout 1962, further dissipating the possible political strength of the detribalized, urbanized elements. Early in May 1962, for example, still another party sprang up, the Swazi Freedom party. Led by Mr. Winston Madlala and entirely Swazi in composition, it was a curious blend of militancy and compromise. It favored majority rule for the Swazis under the ngwenyama, denounced the important economic position of the non-Swazi Africans in Swaziland, and attacked the fifty-fifty sharing-of-power concept. Curiously enough (for the party, lacking funds, leadership, and organization, quickly faded into oblivion), the Swazi Freedom party advocated a legislature whose form and composition closely approximated that provided by the British-imposed constitution of 1963. Seeking to create a framework that would accommodate all three elements, Madlala called for a legislature of twenty-four members, eight chosen by the ngwenyama, eight by the Swazis on a common electoral role, and eight Europeans elected by "people who came to Swaziland as settlers and became Swazis by naturalization." [34] In addition, four officials were to be appointed by the British government. In the all-or-nothing ethos pervading Swaziland at this time, the proposals were attacked by nearly everyone Madlala had sought to placate, which indicated that a spirit of compromise was not yet abroad in the territory.

As if the political landscape were not cluttered enough, two

34. *Ibid.*, no. 18 (May 1, 1962): 5.

other parties made brief appearances on the national scene.
Clifford Nkosi founded the Mbandzeni party in April. Mr.
Nkosi, a law clerk in a firm of South African lawyers, stressed
the past glories of Swaziland and urged the creation of a neo-
tribal political system but one that utilized the principle of
one man, one vote. It was never clear exactly where the party
stood with regard to European participation in the proposed
political arrangement, but many of Nkosi's other pronouncements seemed designed to make of Swaziland a Bantustan.
The ideological stand of the party was further blurred when,
in May 1962, Nkosi merged his tiny group with the National Convention party of Dr. George Msibi. Dr. Msibi had
studied medicine in India and Japan, returning home just in
time to participate in the burgeoning pace of political activity.
As will be seen, he was to become a highly controversial figure,
first being accused of favoring communism, then of working
for the South African Special Branch. At this time, the merger
of the two groups to form the Mbandzeni National Convention was accompanied by the issuance of a rather lackluster
platform reiterating support for the ngwenyama, the principle
of one man, one vote, and a territory-wide labor organization
under Swazi National Council control. Within a short time,
lacking any discernible support, both parties ceased to exist.

Thus, by early 1963 the modern political forces of Swaziland
seemed hopelessly fragmented.[35] There had been no meaningful coalescing of the newly emerged elite, only splintering and
counterproductive competition among themselves. During this
gestation period, the newly emerged political leaders had spent
more time and energy attacking each other, publishing long
ideological tracts in English, and traveling abroad than they
had in working to overcome the substantial advantages already
enjoyed by the European settlers and the Swazi traditionalists.
Those in the British administration, such as Brian Marwick,

35. R. P. Stevens quite rightly has labeled his section dealing with this
period as the "fragmentation of national leadership." See R. P. Stevens,
Lesotho, Botswana, and Swaziland. p. 203. For an interesting discussion of
the Swazi leadership of this period, see John J. Grotpeter, "Political
Leadership and Political Development in the High Commission Territories" (Ph.D. dissertation, Washington University, January 1965), pp. 155–
199.

who favored the emergence of a bona fide nationalist movement found themselves with no group to support. The Zwane forces might have served in that capacity, but the NNCL soon focused most of its attacks on the British; and through its efforts in the labor movement, they eventually forced the colonial authorities to rush in troops, hardly the type of activity the British wished to encourage.

Why did the politicians fail to take advantage of the opportunity to form a true national political organization? It is not, I believe, enough to set out the advantages enjoyed by the Swazi traditional authorities and their allies in the European community, although they were considerable. Nor is it sufficient to point to the eventual victory of the monarchy to indicate that Sobhuza's triumph was inevitable. Certainly the ngwenyama had very important advantages, but the political leaders seemed to do everything possible to help the monarchy utilize them. We have already seen the extent to which many politicians had inaccurate perceptions of their own efficiency. Another facet of their misjudgment had to do with their almost fatalistic assumption that, because political events turned out in a certain fashion elsewhere in Africa, they would eventually be duplicated in Swaziland. Almost to a man, the new political elite felt that time was on their side, that in the future they would be vindicated and swept into office with a popular mandate, that a one-man, one-vote constitution would mean an automatic victory. In short, wishful thinking was substituted for political realism and organization. Also, of enormous consequence to the development of a national movement were the personality conflicts and petty feuds that dominated the interactions of the new political elite. From 1960 until 1963 they showed virtually no willingness to work together for the goals they all professed to want and gave no indication to the average person in Swaziland that they represented a viable alternative to the existing power structure. Most important of all, the political patterns that the new elite had initiated during this formulative period were to be perpetuated in the following years.

This is not to say that the new politicians could have easily taken over the emerging political system, nor is it to suggest that success would have been guaranteed had they demonstrated even considerable political finesse. In fact, given the weight of tradition and the considerable advantages enjoyed by their European and Swazi opponents, it was probably impossible for them to have achieved complete control over that system. At the same time, their political ineptness and seemingly endless repetition of tactical and strategic mistakes undoubtedly gave their opponents every opportunity to maximize those advantages.

4

Conflict and Crisis:
The Colonial Authority
and the Setting of the
Political Framework

WHILE THE PROLIFERATION OF POLITICAL PARTIES CON-
tinued, the British authorities attempted to wrestle with the
problems of constitutional advance. There was widespread opposition to the constitutional committee's proposals, both
within the Swaziland administration and in the Colonial Office; but the British released the committee's proposals for the
Swaziland constitution on March 2, 1962, without official comment. The committee recommended the establishment of a
territorial legislature to consist of twelve Europeans and Eurafrican members elected on a common roll of those two communities, and twelve members chosen by the Swazis by means
of the *tinkhundla* system of local acclamation. Four official
members were to be appointed by the British government. In
addition, the committee called for the establishment of a bill
of rights containing protection for various personal liberties
but also insisted that the ngwenyama be entrenched as a monarch and head of state.[1]

Members of the British administration in Swaziland had
serious doubts concerning the desirability of such a division
of power and made these doubts known privately. European

1. Government of Swaziland, *Proposals for a Swaziland Constitution*
(Mbabane: Government Printer, 1962).

members of the REAC, led by Carl Todd, then circulated the reservations among the rest of the white community as evidence that the British eventually planned to override the wishes of the traditionalists and the Europeans. These reservations included opposition to the federal nature of the proposed constitution, to the lack of political opportunity to be provided for the detribalized Swazis, and to the illusion of power that would be created by granting the Europeans 50 percent of the seats in the legislative council. The British officials, particularly Brian Marwick, were indignant at what they took to be a breach of confidence, although the incident merely pointed up the problems of pushing for a constitutional solution that was opposed by the two most powerful political groups in the territory. In addition, the Hamlet-like irresolution that was to dog British efforts for another year added to the tension and confusion being felt by all Swaziland.

The British did try to placate the ngwenyama as they became increasingly cognizant of the fact that British-Swazi relations had steadily deteriorated. Reginald Maudling attempted to reassure the ngwenyama by insisting that "I do not want the Swazi to regard the proposed Legislative Council as a body in some way alien to and distinct from their own traditions. It is important that they should, on the contrary, consider that the Legislative Council is 'theirs' and belongs to them just as much as it belongs to the other communities." [2] Later, during June 1962, Brian Marwick and P. R. Forsyth-Thompson met the ngwenyama and the secretary of the Swazi nation, Polycarp Dlamini, and over a hundred Swazis to discuss the increasing breakdown of communication between the Swazis and the government. Although the meeting was cordial, Sobhuza II was careful not to commit himself to any constitutional proposals and instead stressed that "the most important issues facing Swaziland are the problems of the land and minerals." [3]

The Europeans continued to use the issue of British "hostility" to the throne to drive a wedge between the Swazi traditionalists and the government and to eulogize the ngwenyama. "It is fortunate," Carl Todd maintained, "that the Swazi have a King who has the confidence of his people and is a statesman of the highest quality. We could not face the future . . . arranged with the politicians . . . here today and in Ghana or Cairo tomorrow." [4] Frank Corbett, the representative from Manzini, agreed that the ngwenyama was a source of great strength and was pleased with the proposals of the constitutional committee: "if we can start off with a Legislative Council without political parties, we shall start off on the right foot." [5]

Given the existing context in Swaziland and his willingness to share power with them, European adulation of the conservative Sobhuza II seems quite understandable. What is less ordinary is that, in a situation in which society was in a state of flux, the colonial power was in the process of disengaging itself, and modern political parties were springing up, such an endorsement did not have pejorative repercussions on the ngwenyama's standing with his own people. Certainly in many other parts of Africa, a situation in which the traditional ruler is praised by Europeans and then responds with an offer to share power with them would have been seized on as a *cause célèbre* by the modern political forces. In Swaziland, despite all manner of evidence to support their claims that the king was cooperating very closely with the Europeans, the modern politicians were unable to use this charge with any effectiveness against Sobhuza. This inability was due in part to the disarray of the new parties, but the resilience and cohesion of the traditional tribal structure also played an important part in dampening criticism. Even in the fact of blatant cooperation between the Swazi traditional authorities and those Europeans judged reactionary by the politicians, the political parties were unable to determine the widespread popularity of and faith in the ngwenyama.

For their part, the Europeans quickly set about securing support for the constitutional proposals. During the week of May 18–25, 1962, the REAC sponsored a referendum for European voters on this issue. Although only slightly more than 52 percent of those eligible to vote bothered to do so, those who did gave overwhelming support for the fifty-fifty sharing of power

4. *Ibid.*, no. 14 (April 6, 1962): 1.   5. *Ibid.*, no. 15 (April 13, 1962): 5.

as the final tally read 698 for the proposals and 19 against.[6]
Outside of the urban and peri-urban areas of Mbabane, Manzini, and Stegi (now Siteki), the European vote was unanimous
as the electorate voted as a bloc in the area south of the Usutu
River in Hlatikulu, Goedgegun (now Nhlangano), Hluti,
Gollel (now Lavumisa), and Mankaiana (now Mankayane).
The British simply ignored these figures and continued to
press for a reconciliation between the monarchy and the political parties in the hope of opening some areas of compromise and communication between them.

Therefore, when J. J. Nquku asked that he be allowed to
address the Swazi National Council at the royal residence at
Lobamba, Sobhuza II acquiesced, although he included all the
political parties in his subsequent invitation and structured
the proceedings so that the political leaders were severely circumscribed. Instead of being able to address a grand rally of
the Swazis, the political representatives were permitted to
speak only to a small central committee of the Swazi National
Council; and then, instead of presenting their views in their
own fashion, they were cross-examined by the committee. The
questions were pointed and probing—name of party, leaders,
source of funds, subjects of which chief, reasons for dissatisfaction with the existing traditional structure, and loyalty to
the ngwenyama.

Nquku was incensed. He refused to answer most of the questions, declaring them irrelevant and spiteful. He did claim,
however, that his wing of the SPP had over 10,000 members
and that these provided his funds at "a shilling a head." With
Dr. Zwane and Dumisa Dlamini on a fund-raising trip to
Ethiopia, the United Arab Republic, and Great Britain (and
which also included a brief stop in the Soviet Union), Sam-
uel J. Zwane spoke for the "new" SPP. Claiming a modest 500
members, he declared that the "money they are using was
donated by freedom fighters who wanted to see African countries become independent." [7]

The chief leaders of the Swaziland Democratic party were
also absent. Simon Nxumalo had been injured in a car accident and Vincent Rozwadowski had thought it unwise to ap-

6. *Ibid.*, no. 20 (May 18, 1962): 1.   7. *Ibid.*, no. 31 (August 3, 1962): 3.

pear as the chief spokesman for a Swazi party. Mr. Sipho Dlamini acted as the SDP spokesman, admitted that there were a number of Europeans within the party's total membership of 1,800, and claimed the party was gaining ground. Dr. George Msibi, representing the Mbandzeni National Convention, was careful not to alienate the traditionalists. He maintained that the MNC stood for the "primacy" of the Swazi people—their law and customs and, above all, the office of the monarchy.[8] The program he articulated was neither modern nor tradition, but his espousal of it served an important purpose: it enabled the MNC leadership to remain in contact with the Swazi National Council and paved the way for Dr. Msibi's eventual work on behalf of the ngwenyama.

The meeting at Lobamba ended with the political leaders and the Swazi traditionalists farther apart than ever. In point of fact, the Swazi National Council had not sought a compromise but rather utilized the opportunity to learn first-hand the views and backgrounds of the political leaders. After the meeting, the traditionalists began to cast about for support, both within the Swazi community and from persons outside Swaziland. Early in July, for example, two South African ministers, Mr. Balthazar Johannes Vorster and Mr. P. Le Roux, spent time at Sobhuza II's hunting lodge at Ehlame. Exactly what was discussed is not altogether clear, but Sobhuza apparently received encouragement in his opposition to the British on constitutional matters. Soon after the meeting, the Swazi National Council called a meeting of the full Libandla which was attended by over 500 Swazis. Again, it is not exactly clear what occurred, for there emerged conflicting reports of the objections of some Swazis to the existing constitutional proposals. This conflict coupled with the reported illness of Sobhuza and his seemingly contradictory views on whether there should, in fact, be a fifty-fifty sharing of power indicated that he was anxious to establish the widest possible base of support for his subsequent political moves.[9] Communications within the tribal structure continued during the summer.

By the middle of 1962, the ngwenyama ascertained that his

8. *Ibid.*, no. 23 (July 11, 1962): 5.
9. Stevens, *Lesotho, Botswana, and Swaziland*, p. 219.

traditional base remained strong, that the Europeans within Swaziland generally supported him, and that elements within the South African government and many of the expatriate firms, such as Anglo-American, were sympathetic to his political plans. This support made it possible for Sobhuza and the Swazi National Council to continue their opposition to British attempts to modify the constitutional recommendations, secure in the knowledge that they could play for time and be reasonably assured of some degree of success. In September this support took the form of a joint meeting of the REAC and the Swazi National Council which recommended that the ngwenyama be recognized as king of Swaziland, not simply king of the Swazis, and reiterated their acceptance of the constitutional proposals released in March. In spite of these efforts it was clear that the British were not about to accept the committee's proposals out of hand:

> The majority plan has the undoubted backing of a handful of influential Swazi statesmen whose views are respected by the Paramount Chief and by the tribesmen. But the hostile forces are not exactly a rabble as it has suited some people to argue. There is no evidence that the officials on the committee, led by the Resident Commissioner, Mr. Brian Marwick, have backed down from their standing point that it would be quite unrealistic to fashion a legislature composed of Whites elected on a common roll and Swazi chosen by some rather cumbersome system of traditional council appointments which means in effect that the Swazi members of the legislative council would be the nominees of the Paramount Chief and his closest advisors.[10]

Hoping to resolve the continuing differences among the political groups in Swaziland or, more likely, to legitimize the decision they were about to make in any case, the British government called a new Swaziland constitutional conference to be held in London early in 1963. This time there was a concerted effort made to sample a wider cross-section of the general population that had been represented on the 1961 committee. The British invited four members of the Swazi National Council, four members of the REAC, and one each from the

10. Editorial entitled "Constitutional Talks," *South African Financial Mail*, no. 7 (September 1962): 241.

Nquku-led SPP, the SDP, the Mbandzeni Convention, and the Eurafrican Welfare Association. In addition, there was to be one general representative, Dr. David Hynd, a missionary. The British had hoped that Sobhuza would be willing to attend but he refused, first citing his dislike of flying, then protesting the seating of the representatives of the political parties which had now formed the Constitutional Alliance of Swaziland Political Organizations.

The Constitutional Alliance was a belated attempt to unify the various "modern" political groups in a united front to oppose the fifty-fifty sharing-of-power proposals and to push for a one-man, one-vote constitution. The Swaziland Democratic party assumed leadership of the alliance after dropping its earlier demands for a qualified franchise and calling for universal adult suffrage.[11] In attempting to organize the alliance, the SDP leadership made definite estimates concerning the feasibility of working with the other political parties. According to the party minutes of this period, they were not overly pleased with the material with which they were to work. They felt that J. J. Nquku, despite his ability to draw on the legal advice of the Ghanaian and Nigerian legations, was unreliable and essentially without a base in Swaziland. In any event the matter was made rather academic when Nquku refused to join the alliance. The SDP would have preferred to work with the Zwane group, but the delegation was allowed only one representative of the SPP and Nquku steadfastly hung on to the title and the presidency.[12]

Nor were Simon Nxumalo and Vincent Rozwadowski enamored with the prospects of cooperating with Dr. George Msibi. They felt that his support in Swaziland was miniscule, that he had reluctantly supported the alliance in order to salvage some political prestige after Clifford Nkosi had withdrawn from the party, and that he was sure to bolt the alliance

11. Swaziland Democratic Party, "Minutes of 10/11/62" (mimeographed, n.p., 1962), p. 2.

12. It would seem that this would have been a propitious time for Zwane to rename and reorganize his party in order to avoid being eliminated from the conference. At the same time, there was a strain of antipathy between Dr. Zwane and Brian Marwick that might have prevented his being seated in any case.

if the London agreements were not supported in Swaziland. They felt, however, that Mr. A. Sellstroom of the Eurafrican Welfare Association was a genuine asset and Dr. Hynd, while he could not officially join the alliance, would work with it because his sympathies lay with its nonracial, democratic goals. And, in view of the fact that over 50 percent of the population of Swaziland was at least nominally Christian, this might prove to be of significant political advantage.[13]

The alliance struck the first blow at the conference. In a carefully prearranged move, Dr. Allen Nxumalo resigned from the ranks of the Swazi traditionalists, claiming to have left because

> We had no sooner signed [the proposals for fifty-fifty] than it became clear that there was no intention to get a real mandate from the people. All they were supposed to do was endorse what the committee had approved. Dissent was regarded almost as treason. . . . The July meeting of *libandla* was farcical. It was impossible for the people to speak their minds in the artificial atmosphere then created. I am not a politician. It seems to me, however, that the political parties alone have made convincing efforts to ascertain the real wishes of the masses of the African people.[14]

Dr. Nxumalo was to become president of the Swaziland Democratic party in November 1963, and his departure from the ranks of the traditionalists at this time undoubtedly gave the alliance a psychological lift and some favorable publicity. Nevertheless, the defection did not change the outcome of the conference; if anything, it solidified the ranks of the Europeans and traditionalists.

The British government opened the conference on January 28, 1963, with the minister of state for colonial affairs, Lord Lansdowne, presiding: "Now I would like to emphasize at the very outset that the British government came to this con-

13. The religious affiliations of the population of Swaziland are recorded in Government of Great Britain, Colonial Office, *Swaziland, 1963* (London: Her Majesty's Stationery Office, 1964), p. 17. For some examples of missionary activity in Swaziland, see Gordon Mears, *Methodism in Swaziland* (Rondebosch: Methodist Missionary Department, 1955); and C. C. Watts, *Dawn in Swaziland* (London: Society for the Propagation of the Gospel in Foreign Parts, 1922).

14. *Times of Swaziland* 61, no. 3 (January 17, 1963): 9.

ference with no cut and dried preconceived solutions. We have no rigid plans which we wish to persuade the conference to adopt." [15] The only record of the conference thus far available—the unpublished, typewritten accounts of the constitutional conference kept by the British government and distributed, one copy to each representative—contradicts this statement; for the British were simply unwilling to accept the previous recommendations of the constitutional committee and had definite ideas about what the new conference should accept by way of a compromise. They proposed a thirty-four-member legislature with four official members chosen by the resident commissioner, ten Swazis elected by traditional methods, and twenty members—ten Africans and ten Europeans—selected on a common roll consisting of all adults in Swaziland.[16] These proposals were immediately rejected by the Europeans and the Swazi traditionalists. The alliance took an ambiguous stand on this issue and continued to press for a one-man, one-vote arrangement, although later, after the conference had broken up, its leaders indicated that they had been willing to accept the proposals "in principle."

Following the rejection of the initial British proposals, the conference soon degenerated into wrangling, name calling, and polemic attacks. Often the British moderators were unable to channel the debate into meaningful directions and the debates dragged on. Polycarp Dlamini, speaking for the Swazi delegation, launched into a series of long monologues, some dealing with the history of Africa; while Carl Todd, in a memorable example of double-talk, claimed that the common-roll proposals would lead to a form of apartheid because it would irrevocably separate the Swazis into two groups, traditionalists and modernists.[17] Nor was the alliance above distortion. Its leaders continued to insist that the ngwenyama's influence in Swaziland could be maintained only if he were placed outside of politics!

15. Government of Great Britain, Colonial Office, "Minutes of the Swaziland Constitutional Conference, January 28 to February 12, 1963" (mimeographed, London, 1963), p. 1, hereafter cited as Government of Great Britain, "Minutes of the . . . Meeting."

16. Government of Great Britain, "Minutes of the First Meeting," p. 1.

17. Ibid., "Minutes of the Second Meeting," p. 3.

The fourth and fifth meetings held on January 31 and February 1 were particularly acrimonious. Mr. Nquku attacked the "unholy alliance of traditionalist and white settler," while Polycarp Dlamini, not to be outdone, referred to "political morons." B. A. Dlamini labeled Msibi a "self-appointed politician" and Mr. Sellstrom a representative of a "nonexistent community." [18] The meetings dragged on through February 12 with no movement on either side. The British officials, most notably the secretary of state for colonial affairs, Mr. Duncan Sandys, expressed increasing irritation at the fruitlessness of the discussions and stated tersely that "he did not want at all to play the thing along and drag it out." [19] Mr. Sandys was inclined to blame the traditionalists:

> because the Swazi National Council delegation had come here with a certain mandate, not as plenipotentiaries to discuss and agree to various solutions. That had been one of the complications of the Conference and therefore it seemed to him the right thing to do would be for him to reach certain conclusions and for the Resident Commissioner to take them to Swaziland to explain them to the Ngwenyama-in-Council and have consultation with the other delegates who had attended the council.[20]

The British did make one last attempt to salvage the conference and suggested that the constitution call for a thirty-two-man legislature, consisting of four official members, ten Swazis chosen by the traditional method, ten Europeans selected on a European roll, and eight members of any race elected on a common roll. The alliance called this unacceptable, and the traditionalists and Europeans also rejected its provisions. The conference was then adjourned with both sides as far apart as they had been when it opened. The British might have been willing to extend the life of the conference if there had been any sign of a possibility that a viable solution would emerge from the debates. Undoubtedly, the urgency of contemporary events in Kenya and Malta also helped to move the British toward adjournment, but it was the lack of cooperation that irritated them most. It now simply remained for them to im-

---

18. *Ibid.*, "Minutes of the Fourth Meeting," p. 4.   20. *Ibid.*
19. *Ibid.*, "Minutes of the Eleventh Meeting," p. 4.

pose a constitution under the provisions of the order-in-council of 1903.

All groups returned to Swaziland, frustrated by the outcome of the conference and convinced that any imposed constitution would be against their best interests.[21] Since the respective positions of the SPP-Nquku, the alliance, the Europeans, and the traditionalists had not changed as a result of the constitutional talks, the London conference was viewed by some as being worthless. At the same time, by exhausting British patience the talks were constructive in that they eliminated the illusion that a compromise formula, acceptable to all parties, could be devised; this knowledge led to the imposition of a constitution, which, however unpopular, at least filled the political vacuum and dispelled the uncertainty that was in itself proving disruptive to the collective life of the territory.[22]

It was not until three months later, on May 30, 1963, in the midst of widespread civil disorders, that the British government released the details of the so-called Sandys' Constitution of 1963 (its provisions were ultimately issued as an order-in-council on December 20, 1963, and went into effect on January 7, 1964). The new constitution called for the establishment of a new post, that of Her Majesty's commissioner for Swaziland, which would take the place of the existing resident commissioner. Her Majesty's commissioner would have executive power roughly equaling those enjoyed by British governors in colonies, and he would retain the right of veto over any of the legislative council's measures. He would be assisted by a chief secretary, an attorney general, and a secretary of finance and development.

21. The alliance issued a long, complicated press release before it left London, appealing for public support and raising the specter of a possible South African take-over of Swaziland. See the Alliance of Swaziland Political Organizations, "Public Statement on the Constitutional Conference" (mimeographed, London, February 14, 1963).

22. For some views on the widespread concern over the "strangling" delay in constitutional advance that was affecting investor confidence, see *Swaziland Recorder*, no. 8 (September–December 1962): 5; *South African Financial Mail*, no. 9 (March 1963): 3; Government of Swaziland, *News from Swaziland* (Mbabane: Government Printer, 1963); and Claude E. Welch, Jr., "Constitutional Confusion in Swaziland," *Africa Report* 8, no. 4 (April 1963): 7–9.

The legislative council, or Legco, was to consist of twenty-four elected members, four official members, and a speaker. Of the elected members, eight were to be certified by the ng-wenyama "as elected by traditional methods." [23] There would also be eight Europeans, "four of whom will be elected by voters on the European roll and four of whom will be elected on a national roll," while the final eight members were to be of any race "elected by voters on a national roll." [24] Franchise was somewhat limited. In order to become a member of the European roll, it was necessary that one be a British subject or a British-protected person or to have lived for at least three years in Swaziland; to become a member of the national roll, one had to be a British subject, a British-protected person, to have resided in Swaziland for at least three years, and either pay direct taxes or be the wife of such a person.[25]

The constitution also recognized the preeminent position of the ngwenyama who was entitled:

(a) to exemption from taxation of his personal income and property
(b) to immunity from civil process in his personal capacity
(c) to immunity from compulsory acquisition of personal property and
(d) to the entrenchment in a civil list of his emolument (and those of certain other Swazi dignitaries).[26]

Furthermore, all Swazi land was vested in the office of the ngwenyama and, of equal importance, the legislative council was judged "not competent to legislate in respect to the following matters, which will continue to be regulated by Swazi law and custom":

(a) the office of the Ngwenyama
(b) the office of the Queen Mother (Ndlovukazi)
(c) the appointment, revocation of appointment and suspension of subordinate chiefs
(d) the composition of the Swazi National Council, appointment and revocation of the members of the Council and the procedure of the Council
(e) the annual Ncwala Ceremony.[27]

23. Government of Great Britain, Colonial Office, *Cmnd. No. 2052* (London: Her Majesty's Stationery Office, 1963), p. 1.
24. *Ibid.,* p. 4.   25. *Ibid.,* pp. 5, 7.   26. *Ibid.,* p. 7.   27. *Ibid.,* p. 8.

Only in the area of mineral wealth did the ngwenyama emerge with less than full control. He and the Swazi National Council had wanted the mineral wealth of Swaziland vested in his office, with the ngwenyama holding absolute veto power over any disposition of mineral rights. Instead, the constitution provided that "mineral rights will be granted or refused by her Majesty's Commissioner in the name of the Ngwenyama after consultation with the Ngwenyama and the executive council." [28] The word "consultation" was crucial because Sobhuza II wanted decision-making authority, not mere consultation; and his irritation over this provision and his subsequent struggle to regain full control over the mineral rights of the country would extend up until independence.

Yet, all things considered, the ngwenyama of Swaziland emerged from the constitution with a great deal of temporal power, especially in light of the contemporary position of other traditional authorities in Africa. But neither the king nor his advisers were pleased with the constitution for, as one observer noted, "It is not a constitutional monarchy of the British type after which they hanker. They want the substance as well as the symbols of power and both are anxious to insure that political parties do not develop in their territories to the extent of their own eclipse by over-mighty subjects; the monarchies which they envision are Tudor, not Hanoverian." [29]

Nor were the Europeans enthusiastic about the form of the new constitution: "Whites are suspicious because they are not given the '50-50' representation in the legislative council which they wanted. There is also the possibility that the electoral system will lead to a speedy African majority." [30]

For their part, the leaders of the political parties also objected to the constitution. The Zwane group promised to boycott the forthcoming elections, declaring that "The constitution is expressly dangerous for the country and we shall fight it to the bitter end." [31] Speaking for the SPP, Nquku insisted

28. *Ibid.*

29. Ben Cockram, "The Protectorates: An International Problem," *Optima* 13, no. 4 (December 1963): 180.

30. *Rand Daily Mail*, June 3, 1963, p. 11.

31. *Times of Swaziland* 61, no. 23 (June 7, 1963): 1.

that his forces would "continue to resist if a more modern system of democracy following the Westminster pattern is not adopted"; while Nxumalo of the SDP urged the formula be reversed so that two-thirds of the members of the legislative council would be elected by universal adult suffrage.[32]

The basic difficulty with the constitution was that it was in essence a compromise at a time when the European and traditional forces and those of the modern political parties were still thinking in zero-sum terms, with winner taking all the new political power. The British, of course, recognized the imperfections of the constitution but saw this as a necessary step: "In announcing the constitution, Britain's Colonial Secretary, Mr. Duncan Sandys, frankly admitted his failure to reconcile the widely differing views which existed. He therefore had to follow the only course open to him—a compromise designed to accommodate as many opposing standpoints as possible, while causing as little resentment as possible." [33]

After three years of discussions, the British had presented the political factions in Swaziland with a fait accompli, a constitution that pleased no one and that seemed to thwart each group's drive for political hegemony. By its very nature, however, the constitution of 1963 offered each faction a challenge to utilize its provisions to maximum advantage. The responses from each group differed widely. The political parties, after initially attacking the constitution for not being sufficiently progressive, eventually agreed to participate in the elections of 1964. But throughout the planning and execution of their opposition to the constitution and then to their adversaries in the elections, the leaders of the political parties continued to indulge in wishful thinking. All seemed to be relying on some deus ex machina who would save them by imposing a one-man, one-vote constitution and all proved unwilling to pull together to combat the powerful forces arrayed against them. Given the provisions of the 1963 constitution, they could not hope to gain complete control over the political machinery of Swaziland; but they could have realistically expected to capture a number of seats in the

Legco, perhaps as many as twelve, thereby ensuring that they would have an important and ongoing place in the political system. They could have, that is, if they had proven capable of cooperating among themselves and organizing throughout the country—in other words, had they been able to utilize modern political techniques to their advantage. Actually, as matters turned out, the Europeans and the Swazi traditionalists worked more diligently and proved themselves to be more skillful in the handling of modern political techniques. It is true that Sobhuza II, his allies within the Swazi National Council, and the Europeans as well also attempted to change the form of the 1963 constitution. But once they saw they could not change its form, they sought to circumvent the spirit of the constitution by competing with the political parties on their own terms by contesting the national roll seats. Their existing power, organizational strength, and access to campaign funds undoubtedly gave the Swazi traditionalists and their European allies important, even critical, advantages; but these alone do not account for the magnitude of the eventual triumph. Only the mistakes and miscalculations of the political parties can explain that.

In 1963 the Zwane wing of the SPP, perhaps the only party with the beginnings of a national following, was in the best position to challenge the traditionalists. Yet after enjoying some initial successes in the trade-union movement, the party subsequently became so embroiled in a series of strikes, civil disorders, and legal problems that it lost much of its political strength and it was unable to fulfill its early promise to create a true mass party in Swaziland.

Its movement into the labor field began auspiciously enough. On March 18, 1963, Dr. Zwane, Dumisa Dlamini, and Macdonald Maseko led a strike at Ubombo Ranches and Big Bend Sugar, located in the low veld. Macdonald Maseko was a former official in the African National Congress of South Africa. He had been placed under house arrest in 1962 but had managed to escape to Swaziland, where he joined the SPP, later becoming its vice-president. Nearly 2,500 workers took part in the strike, and initially it was quite successful, partly because, according to the police commissioner, there was "considerable intimidation, molestation, threats and a few minor assaults." [34] The strike eventually petered out on March 25, when the parent company of Ubombo Ranches, Swaziland Sugar, agreed to look into the grievances of the workers. Little was done, however, and the strike broke out with renewed vigor in June. The management of the company, led by its director, Mr. Michael Fletcher, was content to blame the politicians for the unrest and argued that the strike had faded because there was no substantial economic basis for it.[35] In point of fact, the strike failed because its leaders did not make provisions for feeding the strikers; after local supplies were exhausted, they were unable to sustain the strike. The mechanics of this strike were indicative of the Zwane group's approach to the problem. There were economic grievances in Swaziland; and the Zwane group had the charismatic leadership to call and get support for a strike on the basis of those grievances, but it could not sustain a long period of strikes or slowdowns. The fact that the Zwane group regarded the trade union movement as a short-term weapon that would thrust it into political prominence militated against its developing a coherent overall approach to economic problems; and yet, the ease with which strikes could be called and attention gained also worked against the group's carefully building up support through the vehicle of a mass party. The ease and excitement of using strike tactics—in fact the very success of the Zwane group in this area—ultimately hurt its electoral chances.

Yet in early 1963, the time for political action seemed opportune. On March 29 an apparently spontaneous strike broke out at Peak Timbers plantation and its adjacent sawmill and lasted eight days. On April 4 a Swazi health inspector declared that several of the sour porridge concessions at the Mbabane central market were unhygienic and he ordered them closed. The market, lying at the foot of the main street of the capital, forms a natural amphitheater. Dumisa Dlamini who was present turned the women's dissatisfaction over the

34. Government of Swaziland, *Annual Report of the Commissioner of Police, 1963* (Mbabane: Government Printer, 1964), p. 7.

35. *Times of Swaziland* 61, no. 13 (March 29, 1963): 1.

closing of their booths into an impromptu political rally. After a brief speech, he led them up the hill toward the government secretariat yelling "Africa, Africa." Mr. Jack Elliot, a district commissioner, came out of the government building and told the crowd to make their complaints through proper channels. When the crowd refused to disperse, he called the police, who arrested Dumisa for allegedly holding a meeting without a permit. The crowd then dispersed but returned the next day, 400 strong. This time they were confronted by the government secretary, A. C. E. Long, and the commissioner of police, Major P. C. Temple. Again they refused to disperse, and the officials ordered the police to fire tear gas, an action that terminated the gathering.

The so-called porridge riot, like the earlier strikes, was not well planned and did not achieve any concessions from the companies or the government but added to the general feeling of unrest and uncertainty, which the political debates of the previous years had stimulated. Dr. Zwane used this opportunity and the new popularity of this group, to create a new party (or more accurately, to give his old party a new name). On April 26, he announced that his wing of the SPP would henceforth be known as the Ngwane National Liberatory Congress in honor of the early Swazi king. While this change simplified some of the terminological difficulties associated with the political parties, it did little to resolve the crisis in leadership among the new political elites. The united front that had been devised in London all but evaporated; and the SDP, instead of cooperating with the Zwane group, continued to attack it and even tried to blunt its labor activities.[36]

36. The SDP party minutes for this period also indicate the extent to which the traditionalists were adopting a more militant stance in face of the apparent support for the NNLC. Some of the king's *tindvuna*, for example, were reported to have said, "We are entitled now to use the white man's legal devices to do to them what they did to us, to get our land, to chase them off it and to sleep if we want with their own girls. . . . This is one of the reasons why we cannot accept any common rolls with whites on a nonracial basis. If we did they would become our brothers and it would become impossible for us to stab our brothers in the back" (Swaziland Democratic Party, "Minutes 16/4/63" [mimeographed, n.p., 1963], p. 1).

The NNLC continued to dominate the political scene, however. On May 19, workers assembled at a soccer field near Havelock Mine to hear an announcement by the management that they would receive a pay increase of 22 cents which would bring their wages to the equivalent of $1.00 a day. Union leaders Henry Dlamini, Titus Msibi, Michael Dlamini, and David Shiba called for a minimum wage of $2.80 per day, an end to racial discrimination at the mine, more food, and the dismissal of those royal *tindvuna* whom they accused of corruption and favoritism.[37] When the company refused to consider these demands, a strike was called for the following day. Over 1,400 Africans and 400 construction workers refused to work. The European miners and supervisory personnel tried to keep the mine running but were forced to discontinue operations when two of their men were killed in a blasting accident on May 22. The commissioner of police sent seventy police to the area but they did not attempt to break the strike. Dumisa Dlamini also arrived, stating that "An old established company like Havelock should lead in paying higher wages." [38] The company responded by seeking a court order to ban him from the premises, but the workers then chose him as their representative and he took part in the discussions of May 21, 23, and 24 which produced no settlement. As the strike wore on, the ngwenyama sent a message to the miners telling them to abandon the strike: "No true Swazis would talk to me through the strike STOP If any misunderstanding existed arrangements for delegates to visit headquarters should have been made through Imkewenkhoza Masetele." [39]

The strikers chose to ignore the telegram and to continue the strike. It now seems clear that at this point Dumisa and

37. The *tindvuna*, as representatives of the ngwenyama, were supposed to act as liaison personnel between the industrial concerns and their workers; but they were, as a group, easily co-opted by the management and opposed to the formation of bona fide trade unions which would have reduced their power.

38. *Times of Swaziland* 61, no. 23 (May 31, 1963): 3.

39. John Houlton, *Board of Inquiry into the Trade Dispute at Havelock Mine* (Mbabane: Government Printer, 1963), p. 7. To be accurate, the telegram should have read "through Mntfwanenkhosi: Masitsela."

Macdonald Maseko conceived of the idea of spreading a sympathy strike elsewhere in Swaziland, not only to support the Havelock strikers, but also to present the British authorities and the traditionalists with incontestable proof of the NNLC's political power. There is little evidence, however, to indicate that Dr. Zwane either favored or encouraged such a course of action. In fact, at this critical point he chose to play an international rather than a domestic role, and rushed off to attend the Conference of the Heads of State and Government of Independent African States in Addis Ababa, Ethiopia, a meeting that would ultimately lead to the formation of the Organization of African Unity: "I am writing this on my way to the conference of African States at Addis Ababa. I received my invitation to the conference rather late. However, I hope to be in time for the last few sessions." [40]

In the face of the continuing strike, the British government hastily issued the Industrial Conciliation and Settlement Proclamation and, under its provision, ordered the arrest of twelve strike leaders. The police swept into Havelock and arrested most of the men, but missed Dumisa. When news of the strikers' arrest reached the town, a huge crowd gathered to protest and the police found it necessary to fire tear gas and to move the prisoners from Havelock to the central jail in Mbabane during the night. The NNLC executive then held an open meeting in the African township of Msunduza and called for a general strike in the capital for the next day. Over three thousand people attended, and there was widespread support for the proposals.

On the morning of June 10, with a general strike in force in Mbabane, a large crowd assembled in Msunduza and, led by the NNLC officials, moved down the hill toward Mbabane and the government buildings. They were met by Major Temple, a district commissioner, Julian Faux, and a contingent of Swaziland police in full riot gear. The British of-

---

40. *Times of Swaziland* 61, no. 23 (May 31, 1963): 3. For an account of the conference and the formation of the Organization of African Unity, see Zdenek Cervenka, *The Organization of African Unity and Its Charter* (New York: Praeger, 1968).

ficials told the crowd that they could not proceed en masse but that the resident commissioner would be willing to meet with a small committee. The crowd returned to Msunduza, chose a fifteen-man delegation, and returned. The police kept most of the crowd on the Msunduza side of the river while the committee met with Brian Marwick, who refused to accept their demands. The committee returned to the crowd and then moved back up the hill. Although there had been no appreciable violence, many of the Europeans living in Mbabane became apprehensive that evening when the prisoners in the Mbabane jail rioted and broke free. Most were quickly recaptured, but the events at the jail gave added weight to the arguments of those Europeans who were demanding that the police take action to eliminate the disorder and break the strike.

On June 11 the police were out in force. While they were patrolling the streets of the capital, about sixty men filtered down from Msunduza and entered the compound where the police and their families lived. Police units then rushed back and fired tear gas, forcing the group to flee. Back at Msunduza, large numbers of persons gathered at noon to hear Dr. Zwane, who had rushed back from Ethiopia at the news of a general strike and who now seemed a bit unnerved by the situation. His speech was quite mild, even conciliatory; and when he later called on the resident commissioner, he seemed anxious to call off the strike if some sort of concession could be granted to convince the workers that their efforts had been worthwhile. Whether owing to a misunderstanding of Zwane's intentions or a general reluctance to negotiate under duress, Brian Marwick refused to offer him any face-saving device, and the strike continued.

Despite a cold rain in the capital, the strike spread the following day to Ubombo Ranches and Big Bend Sugar, where Dumisa and Macdonald Maseko held a series of meetings. There was some violence used to enforce the strike. With the outbreak of the new strike, the British administration felt that it was losing control over the situation. The Swaziland police force was stretched very thin, with raw recruits from the training course pressed into service and special constables drawn from the gun clubs of Swaziland sworn in. On the night of June 12/13, Brian Marwick reluctantly sent a request to London asking that troops be sent as soon as possible. Looking back on events, it would be easy to say that the resident commissioner overestimated the danger because, for all practical purposes, the strike had been peaceful, there had been no attacks on Europeans or their property, and it had not spread throughout Swaziland. At the same time, the overextended nature of the police force left open the real possibility that, were the strike to spread to Manzini, Mhlume, Bunya (now Bhunya), and Tshaneni, disorder might have become widespread and the incidence of violence could have increased dramatically.

That the strike did not spread to these areas and to the portion of Swaziland south of the Usutu River was due to two factors. On one hand, the other political parties did not join in supporting the strike; in fact, the SPP and SDP actively opposed it. In addition, the NNLC lacked sufficient organizational depth to sustain additional strikes. Although the NNLC leadership of Zwane, Dumisa, and Maseko was able to energize crowds effectively, the group lacked low-level personnel to carry on the strikes once initiated. Many Swazis were prepared to follow the top leadership, but no one else. Also, the NNLC had made no provisions for a long strike and was unable to sustain its activities for long periods of time. Then too, in rural Swaziland and in the towns south of the Usutu River, the party had almost no organization at all; and the traditional authorities simply prevented would-be organizers from entering certain areas.[41]

On June 13 the first units of the First Gordon Highlands Brigade were flown in from Kenya. The British government

41. Interestingly enough, the movement of some of the ngwenyama's forces on the nights of June 11/12 and 12/13 led to reports that there was an impending clash. This may well have added to the uneasiness within the British administration. Actually, the king's levees were not armed with modern weapons and the ngwenyama was very opposed to the use of force against his own people and, in effect, doing the deed for the British. As long as law and order did not break down completely, the king was not unwilling to have the British suffer the results of what Sobhuza felt was their irresponsible encouragement of the new political parties.

received permission from South Africa for the overflight of
these troops as well as for the airlift of thirty-five specially
equipped police from the Bechuanaland Protectorate. During
the weekend of June 14–16, the British set about deploying
troops and made preparations to crush the strikes on Monday morning. Faced with these new developments, the NNLC
cast about for a way to end the strike without losing face.
Ironically, Dr. Zwane turned to the ngwenyama for support.
He and Dumisa traveled to the royal residence at Lobamba.
They tried to convince Sobhuza that the arrival of the British
troops had altered the situation so that it was no longer a
case of traditional Swazis *versus* modern Swazis but simply
Swazis *versus* the colonial power. The king listened to their
pleas but chose not to see the affair in this light. Just as he
had refused to use his force to crush the strike, so too was he
unwilling to help the modern political forces out of their
dilemma. Instead, he ordered the strikers back to work. Whatever the actual effect of this appeal, the sight of Zwane and
Dumisa asking the king for help was demoralizing to the
urbanized Swazis; and the Mbabane general strike petered
out on Monday.

The NNLC had overplayed its hand. Almost by accident,
the series of strikes had escalated to the point where the
NNLC could neither stop them nor turn their demands into
political advantage. By taking a course of action that put
them in direct confrontation with both the traditionalists and
the colonial authority, the NNLC had overextended itself.
Lacking the financial and organizational strength to sustain
such a long period of activity against such entrenched forces,
the NNLC could not hope to achieve very much.

With the collapse of the Mbabane general strike, the troops
moved into the Havelock area and set up a cordon around
the mine and the town. Methodically, the 600 soldiers ques-
tioned nearly 1,000 Africans; when half of them expressed a
desire to return to work rather than face arrest, the strike
leaders were isolated and incarcerated. During the night, the
troops moved south so that on the morning of the eighteenth,
they were in positions near Ubombo Ranches. They searched
the small town of Big Bend and then closed in with over a

hundred men in the area of the sugar mill, arresting fifty and dispersing the rest.

The strikes and civil disorders of 1963 were over. In their aftermath, the British government moved against the NNLC, arresting all its principal leaders and either denying bail or setting it prohibitively high.[42] Despite the rapidity and ease with which the disorders ended, they were to have considerable and far-reaching results. In the first place, the strike did result in improved working conditions. The nearly 66,000 man-days lost due to the strikes convinced many leading companies to change or amend their policies. A number of impartial arbitrators saw a great deal of justification in many of the workers' demands and spurred the government to develop new procedures for dealing with labor disputes and convinced the administration to support new "political" trade unions.[43] Furthermore, the strikes and subsequent disorders gave impetus to the establishment of a police college in Swaziland and an accelerated rate of Africanization. Within three years, the rather ill-trained, demoralized force would become effective, well trained, and increasingly led by Swazis.

One major political repercussion was the elimination of any further cooperation between the NNLC and the other parties. If there had been any chance for the formation of a unified nationalist movement, the events of May and June virtually eliminated it. The other political parties, which had opposed the strike, now went on to castigate the NNLC for its "reckless" actions.[44] More importantly, although the recent events had propelled the NNLC into the limelight and many within the party felt that these activities were just the beginning of its political popularity, the power of the NNLC was in fact

42. Dr. Zwane, for example, was not let out on bail until August 9. There is some confusion over how many people actually were arrested during the strikes. The British troops held many persons overnight but did not arrest them all. The police force also detained persons without preferring charges against them. The *Times* put the total figure under 300 (*Times of Swaziland* 61, no. 26 [June 28, 1963]: 1).

43. Houlton, *Havelock Mine;* Macdonald Moses, "Havelock Mine Report: Coming Clash in Swaziland," *Newscheck* (Johannesburg), October 11, 1963, p. 24; and Government of Swaziland, *What Is a Trade Union?* (Mbabane: Government Printer, 1964).

44. *Times of Swaziland* 62, no. 2 (January 9, 1964): 1.

at its zenith during May 1963 and diminished thereafter. It was simply unable to revive the momentum lost in the aftermath of the disorders.

One primary reason for its loss of momentum resulted from the legal difficulties that stemmed from the strikes. From June 1963 until April 1964, much of the NNLC's financial, psychological, and organizational strength was used up in legal activities. It was not until December 1963 that the NNLC leadership was brought to trial in a series of cases involving the separate strikes. The first involved the general strike in Mbabane. The government had a difficult time proving its case, and Chief Justice Peter Watkin-Williams acquitted Dr. Ambrose Zwane, Theleni Mbamali, Phineas Nene, Nimrod Dlamini, John Mamba, Dogs Nkambule, Shoe Lukhele, Frank Groening, Elijah Simelane, and Josephy Ngema of inciting to violence. The court held that the strike was essentially peaceful and that violence had occurred in spite of, rather than because of, most of the NNLC leadership. Dr. Zwane was exonerated by the court when it was ascertained that on arriving from Ethiopia Zwane learned that he had a "tiger by the tail" and that he had worked to end the disorders and extricate the NNLC from its position. On the other hand, Dumisa Dlamini, Macdonald Maseko and Philip Katamzi were found guilty of disturbing the public order and inciting to violence and were sentenced to six months in prison. Five other persons were given lesser sentences.

The High Court met again on February 14 to take up the cases arising out of the Havelock strike. Chief Justice Victor Elyan dismissed charges of inciting public violence against Dumisa Dlamini, Abby Msibi, Henry Dlamini, and Timothy Dlamini but found all four guilty of inciting to strike. Sentence was postponed for eighteen months. The strikers who were involved in the incidents at Big Bend did not get off so lightly. In separate trials, John Mamba, George Simelane, Mzondeki Mkonza, and Ezekial Mhlanga were each sentenced to three years in prison for inciting violence, while Johannes Simelane received two and one-half years.

Not only did the duration and costs of the poststrike trials immobilize the NNLC, they prevented the leadership from following up the events with a major organizational effort. The strikes also cost the party the services of Dumisa Dlamini. His various appeals were denied; and because of his earlier conviction on civil charges, he was imprisoned until May 14. This meant that he was unavailable for most of the election campaign of 1964. Coupled with the fact that Zwane left Swaziland in February to attend a conference in Lagos and again in March to attend one in Dar es Salaam, the NNLC was often leaderless during the campaign, a handicap that certainly did nothing to enhance its chances of electoral success in the June elections.

For their part, the Europeans and Swazi traditionalists reacted to the 1963 disorders by viewing the strikes as an incarnation of everything they had feared and opposed since 1960. In a very real sense, their ultimate formation of the United Swaziland Association and the Imbokodvo National Movement was a reaction to the events of 1963, especially to the apparent popularity of the NNLC. These groups did not, however, react in this fashion at once. Instead, they used the aftermath of the strikes to increase their pressure on the British to modify the constitutional proposals. In early July a delegation from the Swazi National Council, including Prince Makhosini, Polycarp Dlamini, and A. K. Hlope, accompanied Carl Todd to London. Duncan Sandys refused to meet with them, and the delegation was informed that Her Majesty's government did not care to reopen negotiations. Later, in November, the ngwenyama sent a petition to the British House of Commons protesting the proposals. As the *Johannesburg Star* wryly noted, this was "one of the very few instances in Commonwealth history where a proposed constitution has been objected to because it had been too advanced, too liberal." [45]

When it became apparent that the British were unwilling to alter the 1963 constitution, the Europeans and the Swazi traditionalists set about working to ensure that they could undercut its political implications and sought advice from a

45. *Johannesburg Star*, November 22, 1963, p. 1. For another view, see W. M. Clark, "Views on the Constitution of Swaziland," *Swaziland Recorder*, no. 14 (March–June 1964): 11–19.

number of South Africans, including a prominent member of the Boederbund, Van Wyk de Vries. Confronted with a news story to this effect, the leaders of the Swazi National Council admitted that they were considering the possibility of creating a mass party with which to contest the national roll seats but denied that they intended to make of Swaziland a Bantustan.[46]

The question of South Africa and the future relationship of that country with Swaziland had been cast into sharp relief on September 4, 1963, when Dr. Hendrick Verwoerd, prime minister of South Africa, declared to a congress of the National party that, "If South Africa were to become the guardian of these territories [Basutoland, Bechuanaland, and Swaziland], we could lead them to independence and economic prosperity far more quickly and more efficiently than Britain." [47] These views were later expanded and published by the South African government as *The Road to Freedom for Basutoland, Bechuanaland, and Swaziland* and offered the possibility that South African territory might be attached to these areas in the future.[48] Verwoerd made it quite clear that the government of South Africa wished to see these territories "fully Bantu governed" rather than multiracial and indicated that South Africa was prepared to support groups favoring such a solution. The British government rejected the South African offer out of hand, while the Swaziland political parties fairly leaped at the opportunity to link the government of South Africa with their political opponents. The Swaziland Democratic party said that the offer "shows the extent to which the traditionalists have gone in betraying the interests of the common people," while the NNLC vehemently opposed the "uncalled for interference in our domestic affairs," and the Swaziland Progressive party called it the first step in handing Swaziland over to South Africa.[49]

As indicated in chapter one, South African interest in the

46. *Rand Daily Mail,* October 4, 1963, p. 1.

47. *Johannesburg Star,* September 4, 1963, p. 7.

48. Hendrick Verwoerd, *The Road to Freedom for Basutoland, Bechuanaland, and Swaziland* (Pretoria: Government Printer, 1963).

49. *Times of Swaziland* 61, no. 37 (September 13, 1963): 1.

High Commission Territories extended back in time prior to the Act of Union, and various South African governments had made concerted efforts to have these territories absorbed into South Africa. A full treatment of this fascinating subject is beyond the scope of this work, but the interested reader should consult the variety of works available.[50] Suffice it to say that, with the implementation of apartheid in South Africa and the inauguration of the Bantustan program, there was renewed South African interest in the territories, particularly in terms of the creation of a number of African-run, nominally independent states under the indirect control of South Africa, on the periphery of its borders.[51] In terms of the geography of Southern Africa, the inclusion of the High Commission Territories in the total African area would have given the Africans 50 percent of the combined territory of Southern Africa as opposed to 13 percent of the territory through the Bantustan program. At the same time, the increased South African interest encountered strong opposition from the British and from the growing nationalist movements in Basutoland and Bechuanaland.[52]

50. For a useful overview, see R. P. Stevens, "The History of the Anglo-South African Conflict over the Proposed Incorporation of the High Commission Territories," in C. P. Potholm and R. Dale (eds.), *Southern Africa in Perspective: Essays in Regional Politics* (New York: Free Press, 1972), pp. 97–109, as well as the works cited in note 18, chapter one. Stevens' views on the contemporary Swazi scene are to be found in his "Swaziland Political Development," *Journal of Modern African Studies* 1, no. 3 (September 1963): 327–50.

51. For the definitive account of the coming to power of the National party, see Gwendolen M. Carter, *The Politics of Inequality* (New York: Praeger, 1958). The development of the Bantustan program is covered in C. R. Hill, *Bantustans: The Fragmentation of South Africa* (London and New York: Oxford University Press, 1964); P. Giniewski, *Bantustans: A Trek Towards the Future* (Cape Town: Human and Rousseau, 1961); and Gwendolen M. Carter, Thomas Karis, and Newell M. Stultz, *South Africa's Transkei: The Politics of Domestic Colonialism* (Evanston: Northwestern University Press, 1967).

52. Dennis Austin, *Britain and South Africa* (London: Oxford University Press, 1966). Ironically enough, the September proposals of South Africa had been preceded by a tightening of influx controls into and from the republic, and on July 1 border posts had been established at twenty-six points including those at Havelock, Oshoek, Sandlane, Waverley, Pongola, Mahamba, Gege, and Tshelibe. In addition, aircraft flying to and from Swaziland henceforth had to be inspected in South Africa.

Although the South African offer was rejected by the British and by many segments of the population of Swaziland, it nevertheless offered the Europeans what they thought would be additional leverage against the British constitutional proposals. During the fall of 1963, some members of the REAC attempted to discredit the entire British administration and the newly knighted Sir Brian. Various members such as Carl Todd and Sidney Gaiger expressed a lack of confidence in the British and urged the REAC to vote a motion of no confidence.

Sir Brian was angered and fought back, speaking eloquently and insisting that the Europeans in Swaziland could not turn back the clock, with or without South African help:

> It has long been fashionable to regard Swaziland as an oasis of peace isolated from the turbulent world. To maintain this attitude now would be little short of folly. Change is inevitable and it is the duty of all to see that the changes made are in the best interests of the Territory. To take notice of developments in the rest of Africa is not to be revolutionary but to be mindful of the ideas which dominate, not only national but international thought.[53]

Although the Todd forces were compelled to change the resolution somewhat, the REAC eventually recommended that the British

(a) suspend the imposition of a constitution upon Swaziland. . . .
(b) in the event of the Swazi Nation deciding against The White Paper proposals by an impressive majority those should not be proceeded with. . . .
(c) in the event of the White Paper proposals being rejected a new approach to constitutional reform be developed in keeping with the wishes of the Swazi Nation and the Europeans.
(d) that immediate negotiations be opened with the Republic of South Africa to settle issues of common interest.[54]

53. European Advisory Council, "Minutes of the Reconstituted European History Council, 1963" (mimeographed by the government secretary, Mbabane, 1963), p. 2.

54. *Ibid.*, p. 119. For a further examination of Todd's views, see Norman Herd, "Carl Todd Looks at Swaziland," *Swaziland Recorder*, no. 16 (September–December 1964): 11–15.

With the passage of this motion by a seven to two majority, the political life of the REAC was nearly over. It was to meet again in 1964 for a session on fiscal matters, but by and large the Todd motion closed out the major political business of the REAC. When the British refused to alter their proposals and proceeded to implement the constitution, the Europeans sought new methods to thwart its intent, forming their own party and cooperating with the ngwenyama to field a political coalition that would challenge the new parties on every level.

There is, of course, substantial dramatic irony to these events of 1963. By insisting that modern political parties be allowed to compete, the British administration set the modern forces against the traditionalists and insisted that the traditional hierarchy would not accept a one-man, one-vote arrangement. By independence, however, it was this very group that pushed hard for such a constitutional arrangement and that ultimately brought it to pass. The Europeans, overreacting to the "threat" of modern political forces, pinned their hopes for political power on the creation of an alliance with the traditionalist that would protect the position of the European community. This eventually had the result of bulwarking the very forces that would eliminate the privileged European political position. By insisting that the ngwenyama and the Swaziland National Council develop a Western-style political organization in order to crush the political parties, the Europeans were ultimately left without room to maneuver; for the forces of the monarchy eventually proved so irresistible that they, in turn, no longer needed European support.

All this lay in the future, however. By the end of 1963, the British had issued the order-in-council that actualized the constitutional proposals; the modern political parties were in a state of considerable disarray; and the Europeans and Swazis were gathering their forces in an attempt to utilize the new constitution to their advantage.

5

The Assertion of the Monarchy and the Politics of Unity

THE TRADITIONALISTS DID NOT HAVE TO LAUNCH A major counterattack. With the issuance of the new constitution, they could have accepted their one-third of the legislature and relied on their alliance with the Europeans to help maintain the position of the monarchy. Instead, led by Sobhuza II, they risked defeat, or at least erosion of their prestige, by entering the national political fray to challenge the modern political forces on their own grounds. The day after the constitution was announced, the ngwenyama declared that there would be a national referendum on January 19, 1964, to enable all Swazis to express their support for the position of the monarchy. During 1963, Sir Brian had challenged the ngwenyama's ability to speak for the Swazi nation, and when this information was conveyed to Sobhuza by the chief liaison representative from the Swazi National Council, Msindazwe Sukati, the ngwenyama responded with the idea of a national plebiscite. This tactic was part of the original plan to force the British to change the form of the constitution, but now it became the opening move in the campaign to pave the way for the entrance of the traditionalists into modern electoral politics. The Swazi National Council skillfully arranged matters so that the essentially illiterate Swazi electorate were given a choice between two symbols, that of a lion and a reindeer. The lion, part of the royal crest of the ngwenyama, stood for a rejection of the constitution; while the reindeer, an animal unknown in Swaziland, stood for the constitution and, after skillful propaganda on the part of the traditionalists, continued colonial status and support for the British government.[1]

As soon as the plebiscite was announced, the British administration made it quite clear that the referendum was constitutionally pointless and that, since there were no provisions for governmental supervision of the voting, the results could only be regarded as dubious. Likewise, the political parties were unanimous in rejecting the entire idea. They pointed out that the British order-in-council did not depend on Swazi ratification and also expressed great concern that the electorate, once having voted for king and country, would do so again. They therefore called on all their followers to boycott the plebiscite.

In point of fact, few did so. On January 19, 1964, over 123,000 persons voted at over 200 polling places. Members of the Swazi National Council supervised the voting and the traditional authorities worked hard to get out the vote. A spirit of national holiday prevailed and they did their work with gusto. Only in Havelock, where 140 out of 2,000 voted, did the people stay away from the polls in meaningful numbers. Of those who participated only 154 out of over 122,000 Swazis voted for the constitution and only 8 out of 1,408 Europeans.[2] The British chose to ignore these somewhat surrealistic figures (which indicated that 102 percent of the voting-age population had participated) and proceeded with the implementation of the constitution.[3] While the massive vote failed to change the form of the constitution, it did represent an important first demonstration of the power of the traditional political system and its ability to mobilize support for the monarchy.

In keeping with the strategy worked out during the waning months of 1963, those Europeans who favored the fifty-fifty

1. Those who supported the constitution were called "enemies of the nation, children of *Mpondompondo*" (reindeer).
2. *Times of Swaziland* 62, no. 9 (February 28, 1964): 1.
3. *Rand Daily Mail*, January 24, 1964, p. 13.

sharing of power arrangement set about organizing themselves for the proposed elections. Late in 1963, a number of
Europeans formed a social club, the United Swaziland Association (USA), whose primary function was to arouse Europeans into taking a greater interest in the national political
life of the country and to generate support for the fifty-fifty
arrangement. Early in March 1964 the association elected
Afrikaans-speaking Willie Meyer as chairman. Mr. Meyer, a
bearded farmer from southern Swaziland who still retained
his South African citizenship, led the association in declaring
itself a political party and promised to run candidates for the
European roll seats in the June elections. The USA party,
while technically open to persons of all races, was in fact a
white settler party, dedicated to the preservation of the privileged position of the European in Swaziland through political means. As long as the party seemed to be achieving this
goal by working in consort with the traditionalists, it enjoyed
the support of a majority of Europeans living in Swaziland
even though its primary base of support lay in the farming
districts in the southern portion of the country.

From its inception, the party leadership was careful to
present the European electorate with but two political options: white control (disguised as "partnership") or black nationalism. The USA saw Pan-Africanism as Communist inspired, and many of its leaders evoked scare stories from
Congo or Kenya to indicate "what would happen" if the
modern political forces took over the government. While the
USA group urged cooperation with the ngwenyama and the
other Swazi traditionalists, white supremacy was never far
from its ultimate goal. As soon as the traditionalists decided
that they no longer needed the alliance with the USA and
made various moves to disenfranchise those South Africans in
Swaziland and to implement a one-man, one-vote constitution, the USA moved toward a more frank espousal of the
South African Bantustan program, even urging that the South
African and British governments buy out European holdings
in Swaziland. At this stage, however, the USA leaders counted
heavily on the goodwill of the Swazi traditionalists and on
the ability of Carl Todd and R. P. Stephens, managing direc-

tor of Peak Timbers, to influence the ngwenyama to support the privileged position of the Europeans in Swaziland.

The only challenge to the USA party from the European community came from a moderate group of whites who, led by Frank Corbett, C. J. van Heerder, H. J. Lockhart, and Peter Braun, formed the Swaziland Independence Front (SIF) in April. The Swaziland Independence Front accepted the provisions of the 1963 constitution and the need for European reserved seats but objected to some of the racial beliefs and Afrikaans-speaking leaders of the USA. At the same time, its followers were not prepared to support a multiracial organization such as the Swaziland Democratic party and were opposed to the tenets of the various Pan-African groups. While the SIF offered something of a counterpoint to the USA group, it was never very well organized. Most of its candidates ran on an ad hoc basis, seemingly united only with regard to their opposition to what they took to be South African interference in the affairs of Swaziland and the general style of the USA leadership.

Far more important for the future of politics in Swaziland was the creation of the Imbokodvo National Movement. On April 17, Sobhuza announced that the Swazis would contest the common roll elections as a nation. Toward this end, the Swazi National Council formed the Imbokodvo National Movement. It had a constitution, membership dues, local chapters, and all the other trappings of a modern mass party. In reality, however, it was only a mass-based party; for instead of national conventions or congresses, all decisions were made by the ngwenyama and his closest advisers within the Swazi National Council. It was the political battle arm of the council and the mechanism by which the monarchy sought to dominate the political life of the country. For all its modern appearances, the Imbokodvo was, in effect, an updated version of the traditional Swazi political system, with its strong centralized monarchy headed by the ngwenyama and the Swazi National Council, and the tribal structure radiating out into society, thereby giving it strong ties to the majority of the Swazi people. Moreover, it was to demonstrate the important absorptive capabilities of the traditional

system, for as time went on the Imbokodvo accepted detribalized Swazis, non-Swazi Africans, and Europeans into its
structure as long as they were willing to swear loyalty to the
ngwenyama and to work in the service of the greater Swazi
nation. This capacity to encompass heretofore dissident elements was to prove of enormous importance, a capacity that
would, in effect, regenerate the traditional political system.
It also made the Imbokodvo potentially the most powerful
political organization in the country.

As expressed in its constitution, the aim of the Imbokodvo
was to reverse "the present official policy which is destructive of the Swazi Nation and its established authority and its
institutions, laws and customs." [4] Research has disclosed that
the initial version of the constitution was reworded in order
to avoid political embarrassment concerning the amount of
cooperation between the Swazi traditionalists and their European allies. The original draft copy first submitted to the
members of the Swazi National Council urged "cooperation
with other political movements, especially European organizations with similar policies." [5] In the text finally made public, the words "political" and "European" were deleted, because the Imbokodvo leadership sought to undercut the charge
that it was conspiring with the Europeans in order to control
the Swazi masses.

As a party, the Imbokodvo enjoyed considerable advantage
in the election campaign. In addition to being a truly national party with an appeal directed to over 80 percent of the
potential electorate, it enjoyed an in-place tribal organization
headed by the chiefs. They were able to mobilize the electorate, to teach the Swazis the rudiments of political activity
and voting, and to utilize the prestige of the monarchy to
engender support for the Imbokodvo candidates. The Imbokodvo also benefited from some hard-headed and effective
political advice from South Africa and, through its alliance
with the USA group, access to Radio South Africa. In addition, owing to the privileged position of the monarchy, it

4. Imbokodvo National Movement, "Imbokodvo Emabalabala Constitution" (mimeographed, n.p., 1964), p. 1.
5. *Ibid.*, p. 2.

enjoyed free use of the postal services and a ready supply of campaign funds. On May 30, Mr. A. K. Hlope, speaking for the ngwenyama, stated that "the Imbokodvo is the ruling party of the Swazi tribal government and has as such full right to use public funds for its own aims." [6] Thus, the proceeds so carefully built up in the Swazi National Treasury since 1950 were made available for the political purposes of the party.

The Imbokodvo National Movement also proved most willing to use the talents of a wide variety of persons. In addition to the South African legal advice mentioned earlier, the Imbokodvo leadership utilized the political talents of Dr. George Msibi. Dr. Msibi resigned from the Mbandzeni National Convention in August 1963 and became involved in a mysterious incident the next month. In August Dennis Brutus, a South African refugee, had arrived in Swaziland and, despite South African demands, was not extradited. It was with some surprise then, that the residents of Swaziland learned that Dennis Brutus had been shot in the center of Johannesburg on September 20, 1963. As the story unfolded, it appeared that Mr. Brutus, together with Dr. Msibi, had been arrested by the Portuguese authorities at the Mozambique border despite Mr. Brutus' British passport and valid visa for Mozambique. After questioning, he was turned over to the South African authorities who took him to Johannesburg and shot him as he attempted an escape. There was widespread comment in Swaziland that Dr. Msibi had acted as an agent provocateur in luring Mr. Brutus out of Swaziland by arranging a flight from Lourenço Marques and then driving him to the border.[7] Certainly these accusations were not

6. Swaziland Democratic Party, "Minutes 30/5/64" (mimeographed, n.p., 1964), p. 1. The other parties protested to the British authorities but nothing was done; the British felt that the Swazi National Council was a statutory body with specific administrative powers, one of which was access to the Swazi National Treasury (Swaziland Democratic Party, "Minutes 1/6/64" [mimeographed, n.p., 1964], p. 1).

7. Although no charges were ever brought against Dr. Msibi, Mr. Brutus indicated his continuing suspicion over the incident in a personal letter to the author dated May 30, 1968. Interestingly enough, while in Swaziland, I was told in 1965 that irrespective of Dr. Msibi's past "the leopard has changed his spots." Unfortunately for this theory, the infor-

belied by the excellent condition in which Dr. Msibi returned to Swaziland after several days of alleged beatings.
In any case, Dr. Msibi's rapprochement with the traditionalists and Europeans in Swaziland dates from this period. Soon
after joining the Imbokodvo, he became personal secretary to
the newly chosen leader of the party, Prince Makhosini.

The king's choice of Prince Makhosini to be the head of
the party was not made lightly. It was based on his service as
a member of the various constitutional committees and delegations and on his unswerving loyalty to the ngwenyama. A
chief in his own right, Prince Makhosini nevertheless was
content to play a decidedly secondary role to Sobhuza II.
The ngwenyama was simply not about to create a powerful
political organization and then let it be headed by someone
who would challenge the primacy of the throne. Loyalty,
then, not ambition, skill, or drive, was the prime ingredient
recommending Prince Makhosini who himself put the matter
quite simply: "It was also incorrect to refer to the King's decision to 'go into politics.' The King has at all times handled
political situations right from the time of his installment. If
he sees the people going astray, he can take the lead." [8]

The creation of the Imbokodvo National Movement dramatically altered the political situation in Swaziland; it gave
the traditionalists a vehicle by which they could challenge the
political parties on their own terms but with the power and
prestige of the monarchy solidly behind them. Once they
learned of the formation of the Imbokodvo, the leaders of
the various parties tried to undercut its advantages by a
series of maneuvers. The Swaziland Democratic party, for example, immediately registered the lion as its symbol, forcing
the Imbokodvo to counter with the sign of a grinding stone.
This advantage of the SDP was short-lived, however, as the
British election commission declared that each candidate
would have to run on the basis of one symbol per person.

Of even less consequence was the hastily constructed "alliance" that was supposed to unite the two remaining frag-

mant, a white woman refugee from South Africa, also mysteriously turned
up in the hands of the South African Special Branch in February 1966.

8. *Times of Swaziland* 62, no. 22 (May 29, 1964): 1.

ments of the SPP, the SDP, and NNLC. Gloriously named the Swaziland African National Union (SANU), it was designed to coordinate the political activities of the nationalist groups "to prevent the encroachment of apartheid and its allied policies in Swaziland" and to end "imperialism and colonial control." [9] In point of fact, the "alliance" was totally spurious. Each party went its own way, insisted on nominating its candidates for all seats, and had each of its most prominent leaders run against each other in the June elections. Dr. Zwane, for example, ran against Allen Nxumalo in the Hhohho constituency, while Macdonald Maseko ran against Simon Nxumalo in the Manzini district. Nquku went off to Algiers to attend the Afro-Asian Solidarity Conference and only belatedly bothered to campaign. The other SPP faction soon split into rival groups led by Samketi and Mabuza. Even at this late date, had the politicians united behind one slate of candidates and worked diligently for them, the parties could have salvaged several seats. As it was, their electoral tactics ensured their total defeat.

Dr. Zwane continued to attract widespread attention even though the NNLC platform was hardly designed to elicit Swazi support. Most of the NNLC's attacks were directed against the traditional structure, an institution in which a majority of the voters were not only a part, but a loyal part. Concentrating on Pan-African slogans and rhetoric, Dr. Zwane presented a series of torch- and candle-lit morality plays throughout the country to commemorate such figures as Patrice Lumumba, a person only slightly better known in Swaziland than the reindeer. The NNLC did have a fairly coherent plan for its version of African socialism (which included plans for nationalizing many of Swaziland's industries and much of its infrastructure) but made no attempt to build up the grassroots organization necessary to convince the average voter that this was a desirable program.[10] The SDP did not go much beyond an appeal to moderation and support for a one-man, one-vote

9. *Rand Daily Mail,* May 5, 1964, p. 1. For a view of the situation by a Swazi student, see Timothy Zwane, "The Struggle for Power in Swaziland," *Africa Today* 11, no. 5 (May 1964): 4–6.

10. *Times of Swaziland* 62, no. 16 (May 15, 1964): 4.

constitution; while the SPP of Nquku stressed sovereignty, welfare, equality, and opposition to South Africa.[11] For its part, the Imbokodvo waged a steady, carefully orchestrated campaign. It assiduously played down the issue of sharing power with the Europeans and, in fact, espoused many of the goals of the other parties, "independence," "equality," and "economic advance for all." More importantly, all Imbokodvo candidates reiterated over and over their loyalty to the ngwenyama and the need for Swazi national unity.

The contests for the European roll seats developed along party lines. There were two independents, Sidney Gaiger and Thomas Booth; but the contests were essentially fought between the USA group and the Swaziland Independence Front. The contests for the European roll seats were highly personal affairs, although the SIF stressed agricultural development while the USA hit hard on the racial theme, indicating its ability to deal with the Swazis and to preserve "the European way of Life." Willie Meyer, in particular, waged a tough, harsh campaign designed to frighten the voters: "It is imperative that we learn to identify Communists even when they are masquerading as liberals and to identify Communist-dominated movements. To vote for the political parties is to vote for the Ghana type of nationalism and chaos. To vote for the candidates supported by the Ngwenyama is to vote for law and order, peace and prosperity." [12] In accordance with their agreement with the Imbokodvo, the USA also nominated three Europeans for the national roll seats, while Carl Todd registered as an Imbokodvo candidate.[13] The other political parties also nominated Europeans to contest some of the national roll

11. J. J. Nquku, "The Swaziland Progressive Party and the Future of Swaziland" (mimeographed, Mbabane, 1963), pp. 1–4.

12. *Times of Swaziland* 62, no. 24 (June 12, 1964): 11. When this tactic gained great favor with the voters, the independents took up the theme. Gaiger, for example, ran almost entirely on a law-and-order platform and stressed his long-standing support for the Swaziland police (Sidney Gaiger, campaign handout [mimeographed, n.p., 1964], p. 1).

13. Todd's appearance on the Imbokodvo slate surprised a good many persons in Swaziland, not least of all those on the central committee of that organization. Todd's affiliation apparently was the result of an understanding between himself and the ngwenyama, because his application was never formally approved by Prince Makhosini.

seats; but with the exception of Vincent Rozwadowski, none of them showed much strength with the Swazi voters.

On May 11, Francis (later Sir Francis) Loyd replaced Sir Brian as Her Majesty's commissioner. One of his first official acts was to reject a last-minute petition on behalf of the SPP, SDP, and NNLC to stop the elections and reconvene a constitutional committee. The elections were then held in three parts. First the European roll voted, then the national roll, and finally the Swazi chose their eight seats by acclamation. Voting was heavy for the first two elections.

The United Swaziland Association swept all the European roll seats as 85 percent of the eligible white voters turned out to give USA candidates substantial majorities. B. P. Stewart led the ticket with 1,129 votes, J. D. Weir and E. G. Winn followed with 992 and 989, respectively, and Willie Meyer captured 983, significantly ahead of the nearest Swaziland Independence Front candidate, G. B. Bertram with 607.[14] The European voters had accepted the USA claims that its leaders, working with the Swazi hierarchy, could maintain the privileged position of the European in Swaziland.

The national roll elections were held on June 23, 24, and 25, but the results were not immediately known owing to the laborious task of counting the paper ballots. In the meantime, on June 26 the Swazi National Council announced the names of the eight legislators chosen by acclamation through the *tinkhundla* system. The choice of personnel indicated the extent to which—even at this late date—the ngwenyama and the Imbokodvo leadership feared a surge of support for the political parties and worried about the ability of its candidates to compete with them. Most of the key officials of the party and the Swazi National Council were granted the safe seats provided by the tinkhundla procedures: Prince Makhosini, Polycarp Dlamini, Duma Hlope, Dr. Msibi, and John Sukati. Others chosen were Mbatshane Mamba, John Rose, and George Mabuza. Despite the many advantages enjoyed by the forces of the monarchy, the Imbokodvo leadership chose not to risk defeat in the regular elections.

They need not have worried. When the results of the June

14. *Times of Swaziland* 62, no. 26 (June 26, 1964): 1.

balloting were announced, the Imbokodvo and its allies in the
United Swaziland Association had won every seat. The Imbokodvo swept all the Swazi seats and one European reserved
seat, while the USA won the other three national roll seats
reserved for Europeans. For the other political parties, the
results were an unmitigated disaster. Only the NNLC candidates received appreciable support, and they were defeated
by margins of four and five to one.

In the Hhohho district, for example, the Imbokodvo candidates, Bhekinpi Dlamini and Masitsela Dlamini, polled nearly
9,000 votes to slightly more than 2,000 for the two NNLC
leaders, Dr. Zwane and Abby Msibi.[15] Dr. Allen Nxumalo
was humiliated with only 237 votes, while Albert Nxumalo,
secretary-general of Nquku's branch of the SPP, gleaned but
60 votes and Jan Sedibe of Mabuza's SPP but 22. For the
white reserved seat, R. P. Stephens of USA defeated Vincent
Rozwadowski 8,947 to 2,601. It was much the same story in the
Lubombo constituency. Matthew Gamede and Prince Mfanasibili of the Imbokodvo drew over 6,000 votes to Frank Groening's 1,799 for the NNLC, while Carl Todd of the Imbokodvo
defeated Johannes Jacobesz of the SDP, 6,385 to 1,955. In
Manzini, where the political parties had expected to run well,
the Imbokodvo's A. K. Hlope and Amos Khumalo defeated
their rivals in the NNLC, Macdonald Maseko and Regina
Twala, by margins of 11 to 1; and Charles Mandy of USA
bested his opponents in the SDP and SPP by similar margins.
The worst defeats for the other political parties were experienced in the Swaziland constituency of southern Swaziland.
The European seat went unopposed to Herbert Fitzpatrick of
USA; while the Imbokodvo's Nkosi Hlatshako and William
Magongo took 13,500 votes to 56 for J. J. Nquku, 28 for Sam-
uel Simelane of the SPP, and 8 for Herbert van Zuydam of
the NNLC. All in all, the forces arrayed against the Imbokodvo-USA alliance were able to muster only 15 percent of the vote.

The Imbokodvo leadership was both pleased and surprised
by the magnitude of its victory. The involvement of the throne
in the elections and the assertion of the Imbokodvo as the ng-

15. These figures and the following ones in this paragraph are recorded
in *ibid.*, no. 27 (July 3, 1964): 9.

wenyama's party had paid enormous electoral dividends. The leaders of the other parties had drawn large crowds to their speeches and rallies (apparently more for the entertainment value of those appearances than for political commitment) but had been unable to convince the voters that they represented a viable alternative to the traditional structure.

As soon as the initial shock of their defeat wore off, the political parties attempted to put up a bold front and again repeated their by now hoary ploy of forming another alliance. Under the leadership of Dr. Nxumalo, the Alliance of Swaziland Progressive Parties sent off telegrams to U Thant, Duncan Sandys, and Prime Minister Macmillan protesting the election results and threatening to challenge their validity through the courts. The alliance proved to be no more viable or durable than its predecessors. Despite a joint appearance at the Organization of African Unity conference at Cairo in August, Nquku, Zwane, and Nxumalo continued to go their separate ways. Nquku was soon expelled for refusing to attend meetings. Zwane, complaining of Nxumalo's leadership, left the alliance; and with the breakup of the SDP, Mr. Nxumalo dropped out of politics. By the fall of 1964, only Obed Mabuza remained; and although he retained the title of the organization, its personnel soon dwindled down to Mabuza and Macdonald Maseko. The petition to discount the election results was rejected by Mr. Sandys. When the alliance brought the matter to the court, the suit was dismissed for lack of evidence.[16]

When the Legislative Council met in September, its members were drawn entirely from the Imbokodvo and United Swaziland Association. There had been rumors that the NNLC was planning to disrupt the opening session, and the British flew in additional troops from Kenya. The alliance did stage a small demonstration outside the government building, but

16. There were some instances of chiefs telling voters to support the Imbokodvo or lose the use of their land, and a number of electoral posters in the siSwati used the royal crest in conjunction with Imbokodvo propaganda. These incidents, however, were not widespread enough to have influenced the outcome of the election. For charges of other irregularities see the *Rand Daily Mail*, June 29, 1964, p. 1, and the *Swaziland Recorder*, no. 16 (September–December 1964): 29. The court suit cost the alliance the equivalent of $6,000.

there was no violence. At the opening session, Her Majesty's commissioner, Francis Loyd, stressed the need for cooperation, and S. T. M. Sukati read an address from the ngwenyama, who was unable to attend because of illness. Its contents made it clear that the monarchy had not fully accepted the finality of that constitution and that Sobhuza II was prepared to push harder to achieve his goals:

> We have come to this juncture in the constitutional develop
> ment of our country only after many disappointments and
> tribulations. We refer to the refusal by Her Majesty's Govern
> ment to grant our petition even after the resounding results
> of the referendum; and the imposition on us of a constitution
> to which we could not subscribe. It would be hypocritical to
> deny that our confidence in Her Majesty's Government has
> been shaken. It is, however, our wish that the relationship be
> tween Her Majesty's Government and ourselves will, hence
> forth, change for the better.[17]

Although it was not immediately apparent, the success of the Imbokodvo in the 1964 national elections and an increased confidence in his political power led Sobhuza II to reappraise his overall strategy. During the next year, he and his closest advisers within the Swazi National Council reevaluated and reexamined their relations with the British government and their need to remain allied with the white settlers. The Imbokodvo leadership now realized that the political forces arrayed against them lacked the power and cohesion to threaten the monarchy seriously and that their alliance with the Europeans, which they had once viewed as expedient, now became unnecessary. While this realization was less true for Sobhuza II than for the younger Swazi leaders, it also became important to be accepted in African eyes as a genuine nationalistic force and to find a place in the ranks of the independent African states.

Prince Makhosini led the movement for a new constitution, one that would lead directly to independence. Although he said nothing about a fifty-fifty sharing of power with the Europeans, the motion passed unanimously through the Legco.

17. *Times of Swaziland* 62, no. 37 (September 11, 1964): 4. In point of fact, the ngwenyama's relations with Francis Loyd were considerably more cordial than those with Sir Brian.

For their part, the USA members seem to have felt that the ngwenyama was still seeking a constitution embodying the concept of a sharing of power and felt confident that they could influence the Swazi traditionalists. In point of fact, their political power began eroding from the moment the June election returns were in.

The Imbokodvo began to build its strength for the coming clash with the USA and prepared its drive for final political hegemony. The first break in the ranks of the other politicians occurred on October 10, 1964, when Simon Nxumalo announced his resignation from the SDP. Claiming that he had decided "to work for wider unity," Mr. Nxumalo declared that the road to unity lay with the Swazi nation.[18] After affirming his loyalty to the ngwenyama, Mr. Nxumalo served as head of the Swazi National Voluntary Service. Later, he traveled to Malawi, Ethiopia, Zambia, Congo (Kinshasa), Kenya, Uganda, and Ghana as the personal representative of Sobhuza II. While abroad, he stressed the progressive nature of the Imbokodvo and its stance of national self-determination and independence for Swaziland. On his return to Swaziland, he was accepted into the Imbokodvo and eventually became minister of commerce, industry, and mines in the independence government. Simon Nxumalo's departure from the SDP signaled the beginning of the end for that organization. In an argument over the existing policies of the SDP and Simon's resignation, Dr. Allen Nxumalo suspended Vincent Rozwadowski "for taking independent action" and later, in April 1965, merged what remained of the SDP with the Imbokodvo.[19] After doing a period of political penance, Dr. Nxumalo eventually became minister of health in the Swazi government.

The NNLC also experienced serious leadership problems.

18. *Times of Swaziland* 62, no. 44 (October 3, 1964): 7. For other views of contemporary political developments, see A. Martin, "Constitutional Aftermath," *Swaziland Recorder*, no. 16 (September–December 1964): 29–30; and L. Rubin and R. P. Stevens, "The High Commission Territories: What Now?" *Africa Report* 9, no. 4 (April 1964): 8–17.

19. Rozwadowski had sent off a long memorandum to the Labor government on November 27, 1964, blaming the British authorities for the defeat of the political parties and predicting that the NNLC would take a more radical course owing to its recent defeat.

During the evening of November 3, Dumisa Dlamini was involved in an assault on some Swazi women in Mbabane. He
was arrested and after a brief appearance in court on March 5,
1965, jumped bail and left Swaziland, eventually turning up
in Dar es Salaam. There Dumisa became engaged in a number
of activities, one of which involved extensive contacts with
the Organization of African Unity Liberation Committee, and
he became a source of some embarrassment to the Imbokodvo.
Eventually tiring of life as an exile, he attempted to return to
Swaziland and was captured at a police roadblock near Stegi
on February 13, 1966. He was then brought to trial, convicted
of assault, and sentenced to nine months in prison. While there,
he had several meetings with members of the Imbokodvo, most
notably his cousin, Simon Nxumalo. Following his release on
November 15, 1966, he urged support for the Imbokodvo.
While Dumisa was not given any subsequent position of importance with the Imbokodvo, his defection from the NNLC
cost it numerous supporters.

During 1964 and 1965 the NNLC was also hampered by a
lack of meaningful issues that would arouse public support.
The charges that the Imbokodvo was working with the Europeans were stale and, it seemed, increasingly untrue. In addition, most of Swaziland was caught up in the 1964 outbreak of
foot-and-mouth disease which threatened Swaziland's massive
bovine herds. The British called out the First Battalion of the
North Lancashire Royal Regiment and the gwenyama contributed the service of several *emabutfho* units. Together,
these forces set up three major cordons to interdict the movement of sheep, goats, and cattle and to destroy all diseased
stock. The total perimeter of the three cordons (one in the
Impala Ranch–Luve area, another in the Lobamba-Mankai-
ana-Helele nexus and the third running from Mbabane to
Oshoek and Waverly) was over 250 miles. There was some
resistance from the Swazis who did not want their cattle destroyed. The outbreak was not terminated until July 1, 1965,
and then only at a cost of over $1.4 million.[20]

20. Government of Swaziland, *Swaziland Legislative Council Official
Reports* (Hansard) (Cape Town: Cape Times, 1965), p. 100; and *Times of
Swaziland* 63, no. 33 (August 13, 1965): 1.

The Imbokodvo used this period to expand its political horizons and to increase its contacts with the rest of black Africa. In addition to the trip taken by Simon Nxumalo, Prince Makhosini and Dr. Msibi visited Taiwan, Nigeria, and Ghana in March 1965. Particularly rewarding was the Imbokodvo's reception in Accra. Despite a boycott by those Swazi students in Ghana and efforts by the NNLC to embarrass them, the Imbokodvo leaders were well received and treated most cordially by President Nkrumah. They were even asked to attend the Organization of African Unity meeting scheduled for the fall of 1965 in Accra, a request that represented a substantial diplomatic breakthrough for the Imbokodvo. Nkrumah also apparently promised to reduce his monetary support of the NNLC.

On balance, these initial trips to black Africa had a number of important results. They helped to show various African leaders that the Imbokodvo was not simply a European creation as the Pan-African parties had suggested and that Swaziland, like the other two High Commission Territories, was in a hostage situation vis-à-vis South Africa, a position the Swazis deplored but could not alter. In addition, the trips exposed the Imbokodvo leadership (and through their eyes, the ngwenyama) to independent African governments, African socialism, and Pan-Africanism in their proper context. The very fact of interacting with independent Africa helped to make the Imbokodvo more willing to make an effort to reabsorb the detribalized Swazis and to adopt new stances that would appeal to them. Both during the trip and on their return to Swaziland, the Imbokodvo leaders stressed the need for "freedom now" and "political emancipation," and stated categorically that Swaziland could not "at this time of our hunger and starvation afford to sell our political independence for the sake of porridge, economic and financial independence." [21] The new international stance of the Imbokodvo continued to attract a number of detribalized Swazis even though its subsequent call for "national unity" was rejected by the NNLC, the SPP, and the Mabuza group.

21. *Rand Daily Mail*, June 11, 1965, p. 1; and *Times of Swaziland* 63, no. 13 (April 9, 1965): 1.

Curiously enough, most Europeans in Swaziland were content to write off the new Imbokodvo pronouncements as mere rhetoric, and the USA leadership itself pressured the Swazis to get on with the business of creating a new constitution. Some alarm, however, was expressed over Imbokodvo's attempts to raise "donations" of over $100,000 and to create a single, Imbokodvo-sponsored labor union for all Swaziland: "Imbokodvo calls upon the people and the business concerns of Swaziland, whether industrial, commercial, agricultural or personal to subscribe to the Imbokodvo National Movement and by this means invest in the future of our beloved Swaziland." [22] European-owned concerns were not at all pleased with these developments and with the idea of dealing with a single union under the control of the Imbokodvo.[23] Moreover, the NNLC and the nonpolitical elements within the trade-union movement also protested the plan and formed a Federation of Trade Unions to stave off the Imbokodvo thrust. Nevertheless, by 1966 each of the trade unions in Swaziland was more or less split into pro-Imbokodvo, pro-NNLC, and apolitical factions. The Imbokodvo was not able to capture control of the movement, but its activities within the trade unions substantially diluted the NNLC's base of operations and greatly reduced the possibility of another general strike instigated by the NNLC.[24]

More frustrating surprises were in store for those Europeans who had banked on the ability of the USA to "keep the Swazis in their place." In September, Her Majesty's commissioner appointed twelve members of the Legco to serve with himself, Mr. A. C. E. Long, and Mr. J. T. Dickie, on the new constitutional committee. Representing the Imbokodvo were Prince Makhosini, Masitsela Dlamini, J. Sukati, Dr. Msibi, A. K. Hlope, Polycarp Dlamini, Prince Mfanasibili, and Carl Todd;

22. *Times of Swaziland* 63, no. 34 (August 6, 1965): 1. Dr. Msibi, however, was eventually ousted from the Imbokodvo in July 1966 for attempting to sell a Swazi National Clinic.

23. *Swaziland Recorder*, no. 20 (September–December 1965): 15.

24. For example, during June 1967 the NNCL attempted to call a general strike but could not marshal sufficient strength within the unions to carry it off.

representing the USA were W. Meyer, R. P. Stephens, H. D. Fitspatrick, and E. Winn. Although the SPP and NNLC protested their exclusion, the British maintained that only those groups that had secured representation in the national assembly should be a part of the new committee.

During the latter part of October, it became increasingly clear that the Imbokodvo-USA alliance was about to be terminated. The Imbokodvo rejected a USA motion in the Legco to give South Africans the right to vote in Swaziland beyond the British imposed deadline of December 31. The USA leadership was furious and tried to change the position of the Imbokodvo, but with the exception of Carl Todd the Imbokodvo voted as a bloc to reject this motion. Even more galling in the eyes of the USA was the irony with which Prince Mfanasibili and others stated that the action of the Imbokodvo was necessary to refute allegations that South Africa was controlling the Imbokodvo. Further, Prince Mfanasibili offered to have the Imbokodvo pay the costs: "if taking out British citizenship costs money, we might help them in buying that citizenship." [25] Since the British deadline would have disenfranchised Mr. Meyer, Mr. Winn, and roughly 60 percent of the USA membership, the USA leaders then had little choice but to urge its followers to apply for British citizenship. The voting issue not only cost the USA some numerical strength, it also profoundly shook the confidence that most European voters had in the organization's ability to control the Swazi.[26]

The USA was even more shocked when the Swazi delegates to the constitutional committee pressed for a new constitution, one based on a single national roll without reserved seats for Europeans. In short, the Imbokodvo was now pushing for the same type of constitution that Sir Brian and the other political parties had sought in the early 1960s. The British officials were pleased by the turn of events and did not protest very vigor-

25. *Times of Swaziland* 63, no. 44 (October 29, 1965): 1.
26. The South African government did seek to reassure those Europeans living in Swaziland that a switch in citizenship was not irrevocable when Dr. Verwoerd declared, "any South African can return to the fold if things do not pan out as they expect" (*Rand Daily Mail*, November 26, 1965, p. 9).

ously when the Imbokodvo stipulated that they wanted an arrangement with eight three-man constituencies (even though the British were aware that this drastically reduced the likelihood of any other political party's being represented in the new legislature). Ironically, the Europeans now found themselves hard pressed by the very forces they had encouraged to enter politics and had bolstered in the first round of national elections.

The USA leaders seethed. Extremely frustrated, they continued to fixate on the anachronistic demand for a fifty-fifty sharing of power and even asked the British to impose such a constitution. When the British rejected their demand, Chairman Meyer then suggested that Great Britain or South Africa buy out the European holdings in Swaziland. The Imbokodvo seized on this as an indication of a "Kenyan mentality" and vigorously attacked the racial and political views of the USA. The demand that the Europeans be bought out and the clumsiness with which Mr. Meyer was continuing to press for a completely unrealistic constitutional arrangement severely eroded the USA's base of support within the European community: "Mr. Willie Meyer would endanger the future of the whites in Swaziland by insisting on his proposals for special representation for Europeans in the legislature. Such special representation must be a minority representation in the nature of things and cannot therefore, as such be very influential. Therefore, why ask for it?" [27]

Other Europeans, including a number of former members of the Swaziland Independence Front, seized the opportunity to publicly attack the USA. Gerry Bordihn (owner of Ross Citrus Estates), Leo Lovell (a former South African Labor party MP), Peter Braun, and Frank Corbett formed a group popularly known as the "Committee of Twelve" (contemptuously referred to by the USA as the "Twelve Apostles"). They rejected USA demands for a sharing of power and called for the elimination of racially reserved seats even though they expressed the hope that the ngwenyama would appoint some non-Swazi members to the new legislature on the basis of merit. Although the Committee of Twelve was attacked by the USA

27. *Times of Swaziland* 64, no. 1 (January 7, 1966): 5.

leaders, it in effect represented the wave of the future; for despite its rhetoric and continuing rear-guard action, the USA was spent as a political force. Once the ngwenyama and the Imbokodvo decided that they were better off without USA support, the Europeans in Swaziland had but two choices: they could accept Swazi majority rule or leave Swaziland. Most chose the former option and relied on the goodwill of the monarchy and their important role in the economic life of Swaziland rather than on any political arrangement.

The Imbokodvo disengagement from its alliance with the USA came at a most opportune time, for it undercut the impact of some otherwise damning evidence that the NNLC had unearthed concerning the depth of Imbokodvo-USA collaboration. On November 12 the NNLC published its findings, including a letter Carl Todd had sent the ngwenyama early in 1965 calling for ironclad written guarantees to ensure the European minority's position in the political life of Swaziland.[28] While the letter did indicate a good deal of behind-the-scenes maneuvering between the Europeans and the Swazi National Council, the Imbokodvo leaders were able to point out that the letter had actually been written nearly a year before and in no way reflected the stance of the "new" Imbokodvo. Actually, the affair gave the Imbokodvo widespread and, on balance, favorable publicity for its disengagement from the USA.

The impact of the news release was further blunted by contemporary events stemming from Swazi participation at the Organization of African Unity meeting in Accra. J. J. Nquku, Dr. Zwane, and O. B. Mabuza had been invited as guests of the OAU Liberation Committee of Nine, while Prince Makhosini and Dr. Msibi arrived courtesy of Dr. Nkrumah. Although both groups claimed to have received the more favorable treatment, neither side was completely victorious. The Imbokodvo leadership had been housed with the official diplomats, whereas the other political leaders were forced to find their own accommodations. Also, the government of Ghana apparently gave its assurances that no further financial aid for

28. Ngwane National Liberatory Congress, "White Settler's Conspiracy Exposed," press release, November 12, 1965, pp. 1–3.

the NNLC would be forthcoming. On the other hand, the secretary-general of the OAU, Diallo Telli, vehemently attacked the three ruling parties in Swaziland, Basutoland, and the Bechuanaland Protectorate: "In Basutoland, Bechuanaland and Swaziland, where we note with concern that the political parties have won the recent elections, organized in *vase-close* and which took place in conditions of which we are aware and under pressures that we can well imagine, are all favorable to cooperation with the fascist, racist, government of South Africa, the situation is no less alarming." [29] Stung by the allegation that they favored cooperation with South Africa, the three delegations from the High Commission Territories drafted a joint memorandum stressing the overwhelming nature of the ruling parties' victories in Bechuanaland and Swaziland (but glossed over the narrowness of Chief Jonathan's National party in Basutoland) and categorically stated that "these parties are irrevocably dedicated to the cause of freeing their respective peoples from the humiliating yoke of colonialism, neocolonialism and economic exploitation. These parties further affirm the unshakable determination of the parties to the establishment of nonracial societies in Bechuanaland, Basutoland, and Swaziland and complete opposition to the policy of apartheid." [30]

The OAU membership was only partially mollified by the joint declaration, and the delegates from Tanzania and Mali continued to press for aid to the "true freedom fighters" such as the NNLC in Swaziland and the Congress party in Basutoland. Nevertheless, some of the more moderate states such as Nigeria were able to dilute the final resolution, which ended up stressing support for the Joint Council of Swaziland Political Parties but without condemning the ruling party. From the Imbokodvo's point of view, this was far from satisfactory, but nowhere near as damaging as it would have been had the OAU attacked the Imbokodvo directly and singled out the NNLC for support. Furthermore, the 1965 meeting convinced

29. "Joint Memorandum by the Leaders of the Elected Governments of Basutoland, Bechuanaland Protectorate, and Swaziland to the Heads of African States" (mimeographed, Accra, October 25, 1965), p. 1.
30. *Ibid.*, p. 2.

the Imbokodvo that, while it and the other majority parties in Southern Africa would have to work hard in order to overcome their images, it could be done. Within a short period of time, the delegations from Basutoland, Bechuanaland, and Swaziland were able to establish themselves in the ranks of the African states, particularly after they attained independence.

In any case, whatever its successes in Accra, 1966 was not an auspicious year for the NNLC. In addition to losing one of its principal isues with the breakup of the Imbokodvo-USA alliance, the party lost a number of important figures in the course of the year. Dumisa Dlamini resigned and Arthur Khosa withdrew from the NNLC in September. After a period of inactivity, he too joined the Imbokodvo and eventually became the private secretary to the prime minister. Other defectors included Sam Khumalo (former head of the NNLC youth wing), James Dube, Tom Abner, and Elijah Simelane. Their departure, coupled with the death of Nimrod Dlamini (who was killed by a night watchman in September), substantially reduced the number of full-time workers for the NNLC and gave the appearance of a substantial shift in support for the Imbokodvo.

Nor was the NNLC helped by the formulation of a new constitution. Early in 1966, the constitutional committee released its proposals for the self-government constitution. The ngwenyama was to be entrenched as king of Swaziland and head of state. There was to be a two-house legislature, with a house of assembly consisting of twenty-four members elected from eight three-man constituencies and six members nominated by the ngwenyama and a senate with six members chosen by the house of assembly and six chosen by the ngwenyama. The senate was to have the power to delay but not to block legislation. The ngwenyama was to appoint a prime minister on the basis of a parliamentary majority.

In addition to his considerable legislative and executive power, all Swazi national land was vested in the office of the ngwenyama, and his status was entrenched along with a bill of rights. Only in the area of national mineral wealth was Sobhuza II momentarily checked. Both the British and the Swazis agreed that the mineral wealth of the nation was to be vested in the office of the ngwenyama, but differed as to the method of decision making in this area. The British felt that the ngwenyama should act in accordance with the advice of the cabinet, whereas the ngwenyama insisted on the power to appoint a committee to advise him on the question of minerals. The British refused to accept the ngwenyama's position at least with regard to the 1966 constitution; nevertheless, following the 1967 elections, they acquiesced to his views.[31]

The committee's recommendations were passed by the Legco in April despite a motion by the USA, which sought an amendment to include a separate roll and equal representation in parliament for the Europeans. The inability of the USA to gain any sort of compromise with the Swazi hierarchy signaled the end of the party as a viable force in the political life of Swaziland, and it did not contest the April 1967 elections called for under the new constitution.[32] With the passage of the constitutional recommendations by the Legco, the matter was turned over to the British, who—despite the valid protests of the NNLC and SPP that the new arrangement was not strictly speaking a one-man, one-vote constitution and severely hurt their chances to be represented in parliament—accepted the constitutional proposals and released them in the government's white paper of October 21, 1966.[33] The constitutional provisions were subsequently issued as an order-in-council in February 1967.

With the issuance of the new constitution, only the April 1967 elections stood in the way of the political control of Swaziland by the ngwenyama and Imbokodvo. The electoral campaign echoed with familiar themes. The non-Imbokodvo parties formed another alliance, then proceeded to campaign against

31. "Swaziland: Poor, Little, and Rich," *Africa Confidential*, no. 21 (October 25, 1968): 7.

32. For a contemporary analysis of this period, see C. P. Potholm, "Changing Political Configurations in Swaziland," *Journal of Modern African Studies* 4, no. 3 (November 1966): 313–322.

33. Government of Great Britain, *CMND No. 3119* (London: Her Majesty's Stationery Office, 1966). As Richard Stevens has quite rightly pointed out, Sir Francis Loyd was willing to sacrifice the interest of the NNLC in order to get agreement on the new constitution. Also, time had been speeded up somewhat by events in Basutoland and Bechuanaland, both of which received their independence (as Lesotho and Botswana) in 1966.

each other. Led by Obed Mabuza, the United Front, including a dozen or so members of the hastily conceived Umvikeli Wabantu National Movement and the rump version of the old SPP, nominated eight candidates including the only European contesting the election, Mrs. Jean Wright. The SSP of Nquku went its own way and nominated seven candidates. The USA and SIF did not field any candidates.

Only the NNLC was able to mount a nationwide campaign with twenty-four candidates. It had suffered an erosion of leadership since the previous election; but perhaps because of this, Dr. Zwane and the remaining members of the NNLC worked much harder than in 1964 and concentrated on winning in the Mphumalanga and Mbabane districts. The NNLC continued to base its campaign on the need to overturn European domination and to establish a government that would put Swaziland in the forefront of the Pan-African movement.[34] Dr. Zwane also continued to hammer away at the inadequacies of the strange constitutional arrangement that had resulted in eight three-man constituencies.

The NNLC was handicapped, however, by the rising levels of economic activity, because the developments outlined in chapter two led to sustained economic growth and gave rise to a feeling of well-being throughout the country. As the recipient of over 97 percent of the CDC's total aid to the three High Commission Territories, Swaziland seemed well on the way to economic viability.[35] The number of wage earners had jumped from 22 percent to over 31 percent, exports continued at record levels, and there was a sizable trade surplus. During 1966, moreover, the production of animal products rebounded sharply from the effects of the outbreak of foot-and-mouth disease in 1965; and of all major cash crops, only the value of asbestos products was down slightly, while sugar, iron, citrus, wood pulp, and cotton all set production records.[36]

34. Ngwane National Liberatory Congress, "Constitution" (mimeographed, n.p., n.d.), pp. 1–22.

35. United Nations Agricultural and Rural Development Survey, *Selected Agricultural Statistics* (Mbabane: Government Printer, 1966), p. 1. The 97 percent figure is inclusive through the middle of 1965.

36. *Times of Swaziland* 63, no. 27 (July 16, 1965): 1–10.

In addition to the surging economy, the NNLC was faced with an antagonist that seemed to share many of its views. In the course of the election campaign, the Imbokodvo issued such a broad and inclusive program that it was difficult to come up with new issues. The Imbokodvo, for example, called for "independence now," a nonracial state with democratic participation, an end to social and economic discrimination, maximum development "in all fields in the shortest possible time," national harmony, localization, increased social welfare benefits, and expanded health care.[37] Also, the ngwenyama, at several important junctures in the campaign, went out of his way to call for national unity and promised a role for everyone in the independent Swaziland.

On April 19 and 20, over 80 percent of Swaziland's eligible voters turned out in the national elections.[38] The Imbokodvo candidates won all twenty-four seats, taking in the Mbabane, Mlumati, Mbuluzi, Ngwavuma, Mkhondvo, and Lusutfu districts by margins of four and five to one over their nearest rivals in the NNLC; while in Usutu the ratio was ten to one.[39] Only in Mphumalanga were the results close, with K. Samketi and M. Masilela of the NNLC trailing the three Imbokodvo candidates by less than 200 votes. The SPP and United Front candidates were humiliated, all losing their deposits. Nquku managed only 37 votes and Mabuza 98. All told, the SPP achieved a total of only one-tenth of 1 percent, while the United Front gleaned a modest one-third of 1 percent. Only the NNLC with 20 percent of the total vote emerged from the elections as a credible national political party. Were it not for the three-man constituency arrangement, moreover, it appears that the NNLC would have won at least two seats and perhaps three; for wherever the NNLC ran well in the urban areas, its tallies were swept away by the larger rural vote for the Imbokodvo. At the same time, while the NNLC had made an improved showing over its 1964 performance,

37. *Ibid.*, 65, no. 12 (March 24, 1967): 1.

38. For a contemporary analysis of the election, see C. P. Potholm, "Swaziland in Transition of Independence," *Africa Report* 12, no. 6 (June 1967): 49–54.

39. These and the following statistics on this page are taken from the *Times of Swaziland* 65, no. 17 (April 28, 1967): 1, 5.

much of its increase came at the expense of the other non-Imbokodvo parties and it made only modest inroads into the Imbokodvo's rural strength.

For all intents and purposes, the 1967 elections marked the capstone in the long struggle for political hegemony waged by the ngwenyama. Having defeated the Pan-African parties, having disengaged himself from his alliance with the European settlers, and having fashioned a political framework entirely to his liking, the ngwenyama now turned to the politics of national unification. Secure in the knowledge that he was now virtually unchallenged as king of Swaziland, Sobhuza II insisted on playing the role of national unifier and his subsequent appointments to the House of Assembly and Senate clearly reflected this concern. He appointed four Europeans to the House, Mayor Mandy (later succeeded on his death by the Reverend Robert Forrester), J. S. Murphy, R. P. Stephens, and a former Labor MP from South Africa, Leo Lovell, who became minister of finance. His other selections included Duma Dlamini and the country's first Eurafrican representative, David Stewart. His senatorial choices included Carl Todd, the Reverend A. B. Gamedze, Polycarp Dlamini, and the only woman in Parliament, Mrs. Mary Mdiniso. The House of Assembly nominees for the Senate included Peter Braun (a European attorney), Mr. Jetro Mamba, M. P. Nhlabatsi, Bizeni Dlamini, and William Magongo. Msindazwe Sukati was elected Speaker of the House of Assembly, thus culminating a long career of distinguished service to the ngwenyama. He was born in Ezabeni royal village on June 11, 1910, and he became the second Swazi ever to obtain a B.A. degree, graduating from the University of South Africa in 1940. In 1944 he was appointed senior liaison officer between the king and the Swazi National Council and the British administration. He was a delegate to the constitutional talks in London, served as clerk to the Legco, and was eventually awarded an honorary LL.D. degree from the University of Botswana, Lesotho, and Swaziland in 1968. In 1968 he was appointed Swazi ambasssador to the United States and high commissioner for Swaziland in Canada.

It was thus a triumphant Sobhuza II who took the oath of

office as king of Swaziland before 20,000 persons at Lobamba
on April 25, 1967. The new agreement with the colonial
authority made of Swaziland a protected state, provided for
full internal self-government, and officially recognized the
ngwenyama as king of all Swaziland, not simply as king of the
Swazis. The shift in power was further symbolized by the contemporary decision to build a new House of Parliament building, not in the British-selected capital of Mbabane, but near
the royal residence at Lobamba. At the signing, Sir Francis
Loyd pointed out the extent to which the present governmental system provided for stability, peace, and confidence,
coupled with more modern forms of decision making.[40] What
he did not say was that for Sobhuza, the occasion was one of
intense personal satisfaction; for he now emerged as the most
powerful ruler in the history of the Swazi people, both in
terms of the number of persons under his rule and their multiracial character. Only full independence needed to be attained
before the assertion of the monarchy was complete, and the
installation ceremonies were not over before Prime Minister
Makhosini and Deputy Prime Minister Mfundza Sukati called
for that to follow within a year.

After the April 1967 elections the march toward independence began. Although the NNLC continued to press for a
new constitution, one providing for sixty individual constituencies, this proposal was rejected by the parliament and the
British authorities. Final independence talks were held on
February 19 to 24 in London; and despite the brief demonstration by Dr. Zwane and K. T. Samketi, the date for independence and the constitutional arrangements were decided
on. Only in the area of land alienation was there some fric-
tion between the Swazis and the British. The Swazis maintained that the British were responsible for the land alienation
in that they had sanctioned the concessions of the nineteenth
century when they assumed responsibility for Swaziland in
1903. The British insisted that the Swazis, not they, were re-

---

40. *Ibid.*, pp. 1, 2. For his part, Dr. Zwane cabled the Organization of
African Unity stating, "Fraudulent bogus constitution imposed by British
on country. African states to bring pressure on Britain to have it suspended. Demand representative and democratic constitution" (*ibid.*, p. 2).

sponsible for the alienation, and there could be no compensation paid to the Swazi nation. They did offer to send a team to Swaziland to study the situation, but its findings did not support the Swazi position. Despite a last-minute delegation led by Prince Makhosini and Dr. Allen Nxumalo in July, independence did not bring with it compensation.[41]

Once the date for independence was set and the constitutional affairs settled, the political life of Swaziland entered a period of tranquility. With the approach of independence, increasing economic prosperity, substantial localization, and a lack of divisive issues, political activity died down. The NNLC continued to press the British and the OAU for a new constitution but was unable to effect a change or to marshal much in the way of public support for such a change. After some deliberation, Dr. Zwane finally gave his pledge that the party would not disrupt the independence celebrations.

On September 6, 1968, precisely at noon, the independent Kingdom of Swaziland was reborn, and British colonial rule in Africa came to an end. With enthusiastic celebrations, the citizens of Swaziland greeted independence and the emergence of the new kingdom. Events had come something of a full circle from the early nineteenth century, since a powerful centralized monarchy led by the ngwenyama again emerged as an independent state. The events of the 1960s had seen the resiliency of the traditional political system, the political expertise of Sobhuza II, and the expansion of the monarchy until it encompassed all of Swaziland. Whatever lay in the future for the country and the monarchy, the reign of Sobhuza would be remembered as a period in which the traditional authorities triumphed over a number of opponents: British colonial officials, Pan-African parties, and European settlers. Furthermore, even taking into account the advantages enjoyed by the traditionalists and the nature of the political arena in which they struggled, the decade from 1960 to 1970 offered an amendment to that portion of developmental theory that stressed the basic incompatibility between "modern" and "traditional" political forces and the fragility of traditional authorities in

41. On the other hand, the British finally accepted the ngwenyama's view of his power with regard to the mineral wealth of the nation.

postindependence Africa. In Swaziland the ngwenyama and
the traditional authorities gained, not lost, power during decolonization; their experience indicated that a modern political framework could be used to advantage by traditional
authorities.[42] In the following chapter we shall look at Swaziland's present position in Southern Africa and speculate about
the post-Sobhuza era; but taking 1970 as a reference point, the
triumph of the monarchy is incontestable.[43]

42. As C. S. Whitaker has written in connection with Northern Nigeria,
what resulted was a "stable symbiosis," with the traditional elite gaining
power and a resultant stabilization of society (C. S. Whitaker, *The Politics
of Tradition*, p. 467).

43. For their part, the modern political parties could well claim that
their activities on behalf of a one-man, one-vote, nonracial constitution
had contributed substantially to the new political system and that, without their efforts, the Imbokodvo might never have espoused such positions.
It would also be fair to say that given the forces arrayed against them
after the beginning of 1964, they could not have been expected to win a
majority of the seats in the national parliament. At the same time, as the
preceding two chapters indicate, their disunity, leadership fragmentation, and poor campaign techniques undoubtedly enabled the traditionalists to make full use of those advantages.

6

Swaziland, Southern Africa, and the Future

AS LONG AS SOBHUZA II REMAINS HEALTHY AND VIGOR-
ous, he will continue to dominate the political life of Swaziland. The magnitude of the recent success of the monarchy
has ensured that he will remain at the heart of the political
system and in control of it for as long as he is physically and
mentally able. Yet Sobhuza is already in his early seventies,
and his very success and continued importance to the political
system calls attention to the future. What will happen in
Swaziland when he leaves the scene? Can the power of the
monarchy, so carefully built up over the past two decades, be
passed on intact to his successor? The answers to these questions are by no means clear. As outlined in chapter one, succession is a complicated business in Swaziland, and the heir to
the throne is not usually or widely known during the life of
the ngwenyama. Even were Sobhuza II to designate a favorite
wife and son to succeed him, the Swazi system of succession does
not ensure that his choice will prevail; for it is the Dlamini
family council (*Lusendvo*) that ultimately has the final say.
When the king dies, his death is not immediately announced
to the nation. It is said simply that he is "sick." This is the
only occasion on which the word is used in connection with
the ngwenyama. Normally when he is ill, the Swazis say simply
that "he is indisposed" (*Inkhosi iyabenya*). It is only after the
next queen mother and her son are designated by the Dlamini
family council that it is announced that "The king is dead;
long live the king!" (*Inkhosi ifile; Bayethe*).

In terms of the post-Sobhuza era, a good deal could depend on whoever occupies the position of *ndlovukazi*. We have made scant reference to the position of queen mother in this work because the present ndlovukazi is old, infirm, and of only marginal importance to the recent assertion of the monarchy. Her minor role is due in large part to the length of Sobhuza's reign and to his political skill. Until he ascended the throne in 1921, his grandmother, Labotshibeni, served as queen mother. She was replaced by Sobhuza's mother Lomawa. On her death in 1938, first one of Lomowa's sisters, then another, were appointed to serve as ndlovukazi. This meant that when the crucial events of the 1960s were occurring, the ndlovukazi played only the most modest of roles. Nevertheless, at a number of important points in Swazi history, most notably during the regency and rule of Bhunu, the queen mother has played an important political role; for in both the theory and the practice of Swazi kingship, the offices of ngwenyama and ndlovukazi are held to be complementary, and the ndlovukazi is supposed to help the ngwenyama in political as well as social and cultural matters. It is in this context that the office of ndlovukazi could take on added significance in any future interregnum, especially if the Lusendvo were to designate a minor as the next ngwenyama. At the same time, given the present composition of the Swazi leadership, it is unlikely that the next ndlovukazi would have the education and the political expertise to play a dominant role vis-à-vis the leaders of the Swazi National Council and the Imbokodvo.

Given the nature of the Swazi system of power transition, one cannot speculate with much profit on exactly who will succeed Sobhuza; but one can say that the next Dlamini family council, by its very selection, will go a long way toward establishing the relationship of the monarchy both to the traditional hierarchy and to the modern political institutions that have developed in the postwar period. It would seem that whoever is chosen, the next ngwenyama will not be able to dominate the political life of Swaziland to the extent that Sobhuza has. For one thing, Sobhuza II had over thirty years in which to gain experience and political expertise before he was called

on to make the critical choices of his reign. The next ngwenyama will be faced with the need to act from the moment he
assumes office and will also be faced with an in-place, ongoing
political system led by elites of experience and confidence,
most of whom have been involved in political maneuvering
for over a decade. It seems doubtful that either the Swazi
National Council or the Imbokodvo will accept the domi-
nance of the next ngwenyama to the extent they have during
the rule of Sobhuza II. It also seems likely that there will be
increased strains within the Swazi tribal hierarchy as numerous
individuals and groups seek to consolidate or gain power at
the expense of the next ngwenyama.

It is in this context that the leadership of the Imbokodvo
will be a considerable force, seeking in its turn political power
in relation to the throne. As a party, the Imbokodvo controls
the commanding heights of political power and regards the
NNLC as only a minor threat to its continuing rule. While
retaining the bulk of its rural, conservative support, the Imbokodvo has successfully portrayed itself as a dynamic organization, the only political force that can keep Swaziland politically stable and economically viable and one that is capable of
absorbing any persons who wish to participate in the political
life of the nation. With the departure of Sobhuza, the leaders
of the Imbokodvo may well press for additional power, including the right to choose the next prime minister. While Prince
Makhosini may be kept in power initially in order to ensure
continuity, over time he is likely to be replaced by a younger,
more vigorous leader, one who will show somewhat greater
independence in relation to the throne even though he will
have to continue to have strong backing from the traditional
leadership within the Swazi National Council. In this regard,
men such as Prince Mfanasibili, minister for local affairs, and
Elias Dhladhla, minister of state for establishment and training, represent the type of persons who could emerge as important leaders.

In terms of the future, however, it should be pointed out
that the Imbokodvo is not without weaknesses. Its present
apparatus depends on the symbolic strength of the monarchy
and the continuation of the tribal structure. Should the for-

mer be reduced by the caliber of the next ngwenyama or the latter significantly eroded under the increasing impact of modern life, it would be necessary for the Imbokodvo to seek alternative means of maintaining its position. Given the present socioeconomic situation in Swaziland, the tribal fabric is not likely to be rapidly unwoven; but the Imbokodvo will have to continue to develop internally if it is to embrace the growing numbers of politically aware Swazis who desire political participation and if Swaziland is to avoid the patterns of political devolution that have occurred elsewhere in Africa.[1] As more and more Swazis receive education and enter the cash sector of the economy, they may become increasingly impatient with the local tribal authorities and want a greater say in the affairs of the party and the country. There will undoubtedly also be strains within the Imbokodvo leadership as the new bureaucrats and the older tribal authorities struggle to maintain or enhance their positions. Heretofore, the monarchy has been both a symbol of and a force for cohesion; but it seems doubtful that the next king will be able to totally control the pressures for greater participation and polyarchical decision making within the Imbokodvo. If the Imbokodvo is to grow, it will simply have to develop the mechanisms for adaption to the new socioeconomic realities.

One problem with which the Imbokodvo will not have to grapple is that outlined by Norman Miller is his analysis of political development in Tanzania. Looking at the organization of the Tanganyikan African National Union (TANU) and the amount of national integration it has been able to foster, Miller concludes that, while the party exhibits a high degree of linkage within the local rural units (such as the village committees), it has a relatively low degree of linkage between those local units and the district and national levels.[2] This problem has been rather persistent throughout Africa

1. For an overview of this phenomenon elsewhere in Africa, see "Politics in Africa: Patterns of Growth and Decay," in C. P. Potholm, *Four African Political Systems* (Englewood Cliffs: Prentice-Hall, 1970), pp. 272–296.

2. Norman N. Miller, "The Rural African Party: Political Participation in Tanzania," *American Political Science Review* 64, no. 2 (June 1970): 548–571.

in the postindependence period. In the case of Swaziland, however, the Imbokodvo is the political beneficiary of the centralized nature of the traditional Swazi political system. As this
study indicates, vertical integration is far more advanced in
Swaziland than in those systems based on a large number of
ethnic units where each is organized internally but where there
are few links to the national center. Even if the power of the
ngwenyama declines in the future, the monarchy should continue to provide a solid core of political and symbolic integration, at least for the Swazis in the country.

At the same time, the expansion of the Swazi political
system to include all the inhabitants of Swaziland presents
the Imbokodvo with a somewhat different set of concerns.
While it has been highly successful in integrating Europeans
and, to a lesser extent, Eurafricans into the present political
system, it has not yet devised methods for ensuring the participation of large numbers of non-Swazi Africans within the Imbokodvo. The 8,600 Shanganas, 8,500 Zulus, 2,000 Nyazas,
and 1,700 Sothos have been somewhat integrated into the
social and economic structures of the country, but their integration into the political system has come about largely
through the efforts of the NNLC, not the Imbokodvo.[3] In
terms of numbers, these non-Swazi Africans do not represent a
substantial threat to the political hegemony of the Imbokodvo,
but they do continue to present a serious challenge to its concept of a multiracial state with the Imbokodvo standing as the
party of all the people in Swaziland. It should be remembered,
however, that the Imbokodvo, by not embracing these non-
Swazi Africans, represents the feelings of many Swazis, particularly those in rural areas.

For its part, the NNLC has consistently sought to have non-
Swazi Africans integrated into the community and has drawn

3. The incorporation process, the method by which outsiders are drawn
into the tribal unit, is just now beginning to command the attention it
deserves from scholars. See Ronald Cohen and John Middleton (eds.),
From Tribe to Nation in Africa (Scranton, Penn.: Chandler, 1970). For
some insights into the general problems presented by the very existence
of a plural society, the reader should consult Leo Kuper and M. G. Smith
(eds.), *Pluralism in Africa* (Berkeley and Los Angeles: University of California Press, 1969).

considerable electoral support from this group. At the present time, the NNLC continues to provide an alternative to the Imbokodvo and remains the only other viable national party. Its yearly conferences draw between 250 and 300 persons, and it benefits from any negative feelings that develop as a result of governmental policies. Moreover, its leadership has remained stable for several years, with Dr. Zwane as president, K. T. Samketi as vice-president, and N. S. Malaza as secretary-general.

Yet the NNLC has a number of considerable, perhaps insurmountable handicaps to its attainment of national power. In addition to the sheer mechanics of the present electoral system, it has been unable to expand substantially its base of support since 1967. As indicated earlier, the NNLC has a long history of fixating on issues that do not command much in the way of support throughout Swaziland. This posture has not changed in recent years. Its public pronouncements on behalf of such African exile movements as the Zimbabwe African National Union and the Zimbabwe African People's Union simply do not generate much enthusiasm from the voters.[4] Interestingly enough, in recent years, the NNLC has found it increasingly difficult to appeal to the more radical elements within its party. At a party conference in 1970, for example, there were widespread rumblings of discontent. Those who favor a significant alteration of the status quo in Swaziland have become increasingly impatient with the tactics and leadership of Dr. Zwane, and it is possible that the NNLC may fragment again. Despite its stability in the late 1960s, the NNLC leadership has not demonstrated that it has overcome the earlier problems of keeping the party together in the face of fissiparous tendencies from within. The NNLC also faces the continuing problem of a lack of funds. The NNLC is hardly

4. At the same time, one does not have to ascribe to the naive and paternalistic notion that the NNLC's support of Pan-Africanism and African liberation are Communist-inspired as some commentators have done. See, for example, A. J. Van Wyk, "Political Stability as a Prerequisite for Development," in *Swaziland on the Eve of Independence* (Pretoria: Africa Institute of South Africa, 1968), pp. 48–68. Van Wyk also exaggerates the military power of the traditional forces in his *Swaziland: A Political Study* (Pretoria: Africa Institute of South Africa, 1969), p. 68.

able to generate enough finances from within Swaziland to keep it going on a day-to-day basis, and it must depend on outside support for its electoral campaigns. This dependence on outside funds could be rectified were larger numbers of Europeans willing to support the party; but the NNLC, while careful not to talk exclusively in antiwhite terms, is perceived to be against the interests of most Europeans in Swaziland, and it seems doubtful that it will enhance its standing with this portion of the electorate. On balance, given the nature of the constitutional arrangement and the absence of any Imbok-odvo desire to change that arrangement, the national political prospects for the NNLC are marginal, although there is always the possibility that any prolonged and serious economic decline or blatant South African intrusion into the domestic affairs of Swaziland could trigger a substantial shift in support for the NNLC and it could win several seats.

What then is the general prognosis for Swaziland? In terms of the economic picture, it seems quite good. Swaziland currently has a gross national product in excess of $100 million, a per capita income of $250 a year (one of the highest in Africa), and a balanced budget. The economy is growing at a rate of over 5 percent annually and exports exceed imports by a wide margin ($67 million to $53 million in 1969). Moreover, the economy is reasonably well balanced, with mining, agricultural production, a small but growing industrial base (including $10 million worth of light industry at Matsapa industrial park), and a burgeoning tourist industry which draws over 200,000 persons annually. Swaziland is a member of a customs union with South Africa, Lesotho, and Botswana and hence has the use of the South African rand as its currency (and the rand continues to be one of the strongest in Africa).[5] In addition, the economic development of the past two decades and the corresponding heavy investments in infrastructure have given Swaziland a firm base for further growth. Throughout the country, it is widely believed that the momentum gained since World War II will continue into the foreseeable future, and the present government is com-

5. Standard Bank Organization, *Standard Bank Review* (London), July 1970, pp. 32–33.

mitted to work toward that end.[6] Barring a cataclysmic de-
pression in South Africa or a worldwide recession, Swaziland's
economy seems to have a bright future indeed.

This is not to say there are no significant economic problems
in Swaziland that could have serious political implications. In
the first place, Swaziland as a whole has not developed uni-
formly. In terms of the intensity and scale of economic activity,
only four major core areas have registered substantial growth
over the past two decades. One is the Mbabane-Manzini-Bhunya
triangle, the second is the area between Havelock and Piggs
Peak, the third lies between Tshaneni and Mhlume, and the
fourth is in the area of Big Bend and Nsoko. These four areas
involve 80 percent of all wage earners in Swaziland, but they
account for only 15 percent of the total area and 24 percent
of the total population of the country.[7] There is, hence, a
wide gap between those who live in these four areas and the
rest of the country, with southern Swaziland being the least
developed portion. Fully 75 percent of the Swazi population
continues to depend on subsistence agriculture for their live-
lihood.[8] This inequitable distribution of the economic rewards of development has already caused considerable dissatisfaction with the present political system and could cause a
great deal more.

Furthermore, Europeans continue to control most of the
country's wealth, and it is the presence of over 9,000 Europeans that swells the per capita income figure to its current
high level. This situation has led to such inequities in the
socioeconomic structure that some writers have gone so far
as to say that "blatant economic and social dualism" is Swaziland's most pressing problem.[9] This is one reason Europeans

6. The five-year development plan which began in August 1969 called
for additional investment of over $32 million. For further details of Swazi-
land's economic situation, see Leistner and Smit, *Swaziland: Resources
and Development*, pp. 87–217.

7. T. J. D. Fair; G. Murdoch; and H. M. Jones, *Development in Swaziland* (Johannesburg: University of Witwatersrand Press, 1969), pp. 47, 59.

8. Leistner and Smit, *Swaziland: Resources and Development*, p. 151.

9. Smit, "Swaziland: Resources and Development," p. 33; and Fair, et
al., *Development in Swaziland*, p. v.

were willing to give up overt political power as long as they maintained their control over most important sectors of the economy. In the minds of many Swazis, this situation is further exacerbated by the continuing European domination in land ownership. Despite the various land-reform schemes of the past three decades, 98 percent of the population resides on but 58 percent of the land; and although Swaziland has a relatively low population density of fifty-six persons per square mile overall, there is considerable overcrowding in numerous Swazi areas, particularly in the middle veld.

In short, there are some grievances in the presently inequitable distribution of goods, services, land, and income that could spark political dissatisfaction with the ruling party and perhaps even the ngwenyama if it is felt that the Swazis were paying too great a share of the cost of economic development. But if this movement is to take place, it will not occur until far into the future; for at the present time, it is precisely those Swazis who are on the lowest rungs of the socioeconomic ladder who have most fervently supported the king and the Imbokodvo. Rather it is those Swazis and non-Swazi Africans who move into the cities and become absorbed into the cash sector of the economy who continue to constitute a potential pool of support for the NNLC or any future offshoot of it. If the wealth accruing from economic development is not more widely and more equitably dispersed, the political system will face increasing stress in the future; however, it seems highly unlikely that any dissatisfaction with the socioeconomic arrangement in Swaziland will be translated into political opposition of a significant magnitude to threaten the Imbokodvo's hold on the national government.

Swaziland's economic situation also calls attention to its position in the Southern African subsystem. As a tiny, land-locked country with a small population and a very limited internal market, it is highly dependent on international actors for its markets and capital. Moreover, Swaziland is susceptible to outside pressures. The Swazi leadership is highly conscious of this vulnerability, weakness, and defenselessness. As Zonke Khumalo, minister of state for foreign affairs, has put it, "We are surrounded by powerful neighbors and no one will come to our rescue if these powers decide to remove Swaziland." [10] Whether or not this is an exaggerated view of the situation, it is a view widely shared by the present Swazi leadership and one that, together with Swaziland's history, goes a long way to explain why the Swazis are currently not challenging the status quo throughout the subsystem even though that subsystem is dominated by South Africa and other racial minority governments.[11] The Swazis feel they cannot appreciably change the situation and that any attempt on their part would jeopardize what prosperity and independence they have been able to attain.

In terms of Swaziland's interaction with other national units, South Africa is of prime importance; and it seems likely to remain the most important international actor for the Swazis into the foreseeable future. Geographically, Swaziland is almost surrounded by South Africa, and most of its major lines of communication and transportation go out through the Republic. Telephone, telex, and postal communication lines run through South Africa, as do most forms of surface transportation and Swazi Airlines (which operates in conjunction with South African Airways). The only exceptions to this are the railroad and roads through Mozambique (and the possibility of regular flights to Malawi and Zambia which are currently being explored).

The economic life of Swaziland is intrinsically bound up with South Africa. Swaziland, along with Botswana and Lesotho, belong to the South African customs union and use South African currency and central banking facilities. Moreover, these patterns of interaction are of long-standing duration.

10. *Times of Swaziland* 68, no. 31 (July 31, 1970): 3.

11. In terms of the subsystem operative in Southern Africa, see C. P. Potholm and Richard Dale (eds.), *Southern Africa in Perspective: Essays in Regional Politics* (New York: Free Press, 1972); Peter Robson, "Economic Integration in Southern Africa," *Journal of Modern African Studies* 5, no. 4 (December 1967): 469–490; P. Smit and E. J. van der Merwe, "Economic Co-operation in Southern Africa," *Journal of Geography* (Stellenbosch) 3, no. 3 (September 1968): 279–294; Eschel Rhoodie, *The Third Africa* (New York: Twin Circle, 1968); and Larry W. Bowman's seminal "The Subordinate State System of Southern Africa," *International Studies Quarterly* 12, no. 3 (September 1968): 231–261.

Since 1910 the three former High Commission Territories have been closely tied to South Africa through a customs union that provided for a common external tariff and the free interchange of goods manufactured within the four countries. Each state was also allocated a percentage of the customs duties. South Africa was not only the most important member of the group, it was the main beneficiary of the arrangement which helped to pay for South African farm subsidies and provided extensive protection for South African industries in exchange for very small amounts of returned customs duties.[12] Swaziland's share, during this period, for example, was only slightly more than one-half of 1 percent.

The initial customs agreement lasted sixty years and was renegotiated as the three territories approached independence. In line with South Africa's new outward foreign policy and its desire to keep the three territories firmly within the South African orbit, the new union provides more favorable terms for Lesotho, Botswana, and Swaziland, both with regard to the protection of infant industries in the three territories and in terms of their share of the revenues.[13] In the case of Swaziland, there was such a dramatic increase in the yearly revenues accruing to it that Swaziland was able to balance its budget for the fiscal year 1970/1971, and should be able to do so into the foreseeable future.

Despite the developments of the past two decades, South Africa continues to be an enormously important factor in the economy of Swaziland. Swaziland depends on South Africa for over 80 percent of its imports and sends 20 percent of its exports, primarily cattle products and asbestos, to South Africa. Many South African firms have subsidiary plants in Swaziland, and private venture capital from South Africa has

12. Standard Bank Organization, *Standard Bank Review*, July 1970, pp. 7–10.

13. Distribution of the funds generated by the customs pool will be determined on the basis of a complete formula involving the production and consumption of duty goods as well as by the amount of import duties generated; Governments of Swaziland, Botswana, Lesotho, and South Africa, *Customs Agreement Between the Governments of Swaziland, Botswana, Lesotho, and South Africa* (Mbabane: Swaziland Government Gazette, 1969).

been substantial, amounting to over one-third of the total investment of $120 million between 1960 and 1966.[14] Moreover, thirty thousand Swazis, primarily from the southern portion of the country, work in South Africa, both in the mines of the Rand and on farms in Natal and the Transvaal. The integration of their respective economies is continuing. For example, by 1972 Swaziland's electric power net will be fully integrated into that of South Africa, a feasibility study is being undertaken to examine the possibility of extending a rail line from South Africa into Swaziland, and there is already increased cooperation with regard to the use of common water resources. The new Strijdom dam on the Pongola River in Natal, for example, will create a large lake that will back up five miles into Swaziland, covering over 2,000 acres. South Africa has also served notice that it hopes to keep Swaziland within its economic orbit as much as possible. During 1970, an American firm, Intermedia, sought a license for a commercial radio station in Swaziland. The South Africans put considerable pressure on the Swazi government to refuse the license, and it was only after countervailing pressure from the United States that the license was granted.

At the same time, it should be remembered that in terms of Swazi–South African relations, South Africa does not enjoy unlimited political leverage over Swaziland. Since 1963, there has been a shift away from the notion of incorporating Swaziland (or Lesotho or Botswana) into South Africa as a Bantustan. Instead, South Africa seems to be trying to move the Bantustans toward the status of the three former High Commission Territories: militarily weak, economically dependent, and yet politically "independent." Obviously, South Africa has the military and economic power to dictate its will in a number of areas; but the international standing of Lesotho, Botswana, and the Swaziland place some limits in African behavior. Since 1966, at least, South Africa has stressed noninterference and good neighborliness rather than direct control.[15]

14. Leistner and Smit, *Swaziland: Resources and Development*, p. 89. The percentage is even higher if one adds the input of such "international" companies as Anglo-American.

15. Amry Vandenbosch, *South Africa and the World: The Foreign*

South Africa now seems prepared to tolerate a good deal of freedom on the part of Swaziland so long as Swazi policy does not threaten the core values of the ruling minority in South Africa.[16]

The actual amount of South African influence on the government of Swaziland, however, is masked by a number of general areas of agreement which result in a real confluence of policy on several levels. As has been reiterated elsewhere in this study, the Swazi oppose apartheid and wish to see African majority rule in South Africa. But they feel that they are powerless to affect such a change and see little point in pretending otherwise. They have, thus, fallen back on a two-pronged strategy: one is to push for greater economic cooperation with South Africa; the other is the oft-expressed hope that Swaziland, as a multiracial society, will serve as an example to white South Africa and thereby indirectly ameliorate the lot of non-Europeans in South Africa.

But this is as far as the present government of Swaziland is prepared to go. The Swazis, like the European South Africans, oppose revolutionary change and feel that any violence in Southern Africa is likely to adversely affect their economic and political situation. Thus, the South Africans and the Swazis are, of the moment at least, committed to the status quo, and Swaziland has been unwilling to provide much assistance for the various African exile movements. This means, among other things, that Swaziland has not been overly receptive to refugees from South Africa and Mozambique. Part of this stance has to do with the internal dynamics of Swaziland. To many Swazis, the refugee represents something of a threat, which is especially felt in the economic sector; many of the refugees have skills that enable them to get good jobs, thereby, it is felt, depriving Swazis of numerous opportunities. Also, the refugees tend to be politically active and not on behalf of the Imbokodvo. Since 1960, large numbers of them have

Policy of Apartheid (Lexington: University Press of Kentucky, 1970); and J. E. Spence, *Republic Under Pressure: A Study of South African Foreign Policy* (London: Oxford University Press, 1965).

16. For example, South Africa is reluctant to have South African teams compete in international sports events within Swaziland.

supported and worked for the SPP, SDP, United Front, and NNLC. One direct result of this support has been that the government of Swaziland, its rhetoric notwithstanding, has simply forced a number of refugees to leave the country. Since 1966, for example, over 1,212 refugees have been declared "prohibited immigrants" and 1,024 have been deported, mostly to Zambia or Tanzania.[17]

Another dimension of the Swazi position is South Africa's long-demonstrated ability to penetrate Swaziland in order to capture or recapture refugees. This was the case even when Great Britain had international responsibility for the territorial integrity of Swaziland. On numerous occasions, refugees simply disappeared from Swaziland. In 1964, for example, the South African Institute of Race Relations reported that Rosemary Wentzel, a political refugee from South Africa, had been abducted from within Swaziland.[18] A series of incidents during 1965 further underscored the vulnerability of Swaziland. South African police, often in uniform, appeared at various places throughout Swaziland and in at least one instance forceably removed a suspect from Swaziland.[19] Nor was this activity confined to South African refugees. Elements of the South African security forces were also apparently involved in the disappearance on the night of May 8/9, 1965, of over sixty refugees from Mozambique who were living outside of Mbabane. Exact details are difficult to come by; but the next day, the group, including numerous women and children, turned up in South African hands in the Transvaal and were eventually shipped by railroad car to the Portuguese prison at Mabalane, 160 miles north of Lourenço Marques. Despite British protests, the refugees were not returned; and the leader of the group, Mario Mondlane, was himself abducted the fol-

17. *Times of Swaziland* 67, no. 43 (October 31, 1969): 1. More recently, this policy has been applied to refugees from Lesotho as well. Following the coup in Lesotho, Lebenya Chakela, president of the opposition Basutoland Congress Party Youth League, was declared an "undesirable refugee" in October 1970.

18. Muriel Horrell (compiler), *A Survey of Race Relations in South Africa* (Johannesburg: South African Institute of Race Relations, 1964), p. 77.

19. *Johannesburg Star*, November 4, 1965, p. 3.

lowing August.[20] Although the number of refugees from South Africa declined in the late 1960s, South African security forces continued to operate in Swaziland and there was widespread belief in the country that South African intelligence personnel received at least some help from the Swaziland police.[21]

Nevertheless, the South Africans have tried to avoid any blatant interference in the domestic affairs of Swaziland and generally have sought to portray themselves as friends of the Swazis, sending technical and medical assistance in times of crisis (such as the outbreak of foot-and-mouth disease) and providing aid for specific projects (South Africa pays the cost of training some municipal and town officials). While Swaziland has not exchanged ambassadors with South Africa, there is a good deal of telephone diplomacy between Mbabane and Pretoria. In return for South African aid, Swaziland has muted its criticism of South Africa in the United Nations and the Organization of African Unity. Despite highly publicized attacks on the present government of Rhodesia, the leaders of Swaziland have not publicly attacked South Africa since independence. In short, the Swazis have accepted what they take to be the realities of the situation and have tried to turn their dependence on South Africa to their own advantage.

Swaziland's degree of dependence on South Africa lies somewhere between that of Lesotho and that of Botswana.[22] It is not completely surrounded by South Africa, as is Lesotho, but it lacks a common border with an African-controlled state, which Botswana enjoys. No matter how small or how contested is Botswana's common frontier with Zambia at Kazungula, it represents an important opening to the north and a highly visible link with black Africa. In the future, Swaziland might

20. Ironically, his disappearance coincided with the opening of the Portuguese consulate in Mbabane.

21. On January 10, 1970, for example, Mrs. R. B. Ndzila, wife of the Pan-African Congress leader, was arrested at the Oshoek border point by South Africans and detained indefinitely. In addition, an extradition treaty with South Africa has been operative since the summer of 1968. See also Kenneth W. Grundy, "The 'Southern Border' of Africa," in C. G. Widstrand (ed.), *African Boundary Problems* (Uppsala: The Scandinavian Institute of African Studies, 1969).

22. C. P. Potholm, "The Protectorates, the O.A.U., and South Africa," *International Journal* 22, no. 1 (winter 1966–1967): 68–72.

possibly enjoy such a frontier with an independent Mozambique; but for the moment, the Swazis do not have a direct outlet to black Africa. At the same time, Swaziland does not depend on the export of migrant labor to South Africa to the extent that Lesotho and Botswana do, although it lacks the long-term possibility that Botswana enjoys of being able to reorient much of its trade toward east and central Africa and does not enjoy the same amount of potential leverage with regard to South Africa. Also, although Swaziland is currently the richest of the three territories, extensive deposits of nickel, copper, and diamonds offer Botswana the hope that it may eventually surpass Swaziland in terms of per capita income and economic viability.

There is very little interaction between Swaziland and the other former High Commission Territories. This lack of interaction has a long history. Although the three territories were lumped together for administrative purposes beginning in 1907, there have never been extensive contacts or significant amounts of trade among them. What they share is a common history of resisting the encroachments of various South African governments and of appealing to Great Britain to prevent their incorporation into South Africa. With independence, however, and Great Britain's disengagement from the area, they have tended to look toward black Africa (through the Organization of African Unity) and the world (through the United Nations) to guarantee their independence and, in the case of the latter, to provide development funds.

There has been an increase in diplomatic contacts and state visits since independence. During 1969–1970, for example, the queen mother of Lesotho, Mabereng Seeiso, visited Swaziland amid great pomp and circumstance; and Sir Seretse Khama, the president of Botswana, presented degrees at Swazi Agricultural College at Luyengo. At the same time, although the delegations from Swaziland, Lesotho, and Botswana often confer on common strategy at meetings of the Commonwealth, UN, and OAU, these links have not been formalized and tend to be ad hoc and reactive in character. The three territories do not exchange ambassadors. Despite all the rhetoric about cooperation among the three territories, each state essentially goes its own way. There is virtually no trade among them, no population exchanges and very little in the way of functional cooperation in such areas as transportation or communications. They do share a common educational facility at the University of Botswana, Lesotho, and Swaziland at Roma, Lesotho (with an agricultural branch in Swaziland); but with the exception of providing some common training for public servants, there is virtually no ongoing interaction among them and no impetus for multinational cooperation in the form of a federation.

In addition to the geographical, logistical, and economic barriers to greater interaction, there is also the restraint of differing internal political situations. While all three political systems began functioning at independence as democratically elected multiparty systems, each has gone off in a different direction since then. The government of Lesotho, headed by Chief Lebua Jonathan and his National party, has never enjoyed the levels of popular support elicited by the governments of Botswana and Swaziland; and it now seems clear that Jonathan's government was actually voted out of office prior to the January 1970 coup it instigated. The coup enabled Jonathan to stay in power but at a considerable cost in terms of international credibility.[23] Privately, the Swazi leaders were disappointed and somewhat embarrassed by the course of events, although they have continued to support the government in power and the Swazis have not been overly receptive to refugees from Lesotho, particularly those belonging to the

23. For an excellent analysis of the contemporary political system in Lesotho and the paucity of options available to any government, see Richard Weisfelder, "Lesotho: The Politics of Desperation," *Southern Africa in Perspective* (New York: Free Press, 1972). Other works which provide background material are Weisfelder's earlier "Power Struggle in Lesotho," *African Report* 12, no. 1 (January 1967): 5–13; J. E. Spence, *Lesotho: The Politics of Dependence* (London: Oxford University Press, 1968); A. J. van Wyk, *Lesotho: A Political Survey* (Pretoria: Africa Institute of South Africa, 1967); Stevens, *Lesotho, Botswana, and Swaziland*, pp. 16–109; Halpern, *South Africa's Hostages*, pp. 135–260; and B. M. Khaketla, *Lesotho 1970* (Berkeley and Los Angeles: University of California Press, 1972).

banned Congress party of Ntsu Mokhehle. At the same time, this political dimension has further diminished meaningful cooperation between Swaziland and Lesotho.

The situation with regard to Botswana is slightly different. The government of Sir Seretse Khama and his ruling Botswana Democratic party enjoys good standing in the international community and Sir Seretse is probably the most highly regarded of the three national leaders.[24] The Botswana have a functioning multiparty system; and because of the one-man, one-vote constitutional arrangement, one-third of the seats in the parliament are held by the opposition Botswana People's party, the Botswana Independence party, and the Botswana National Front. Although the government currently controls with a two-thirds majority, it has to face a number of difficult problems on which the opposition is quick to capitalize.[25] The very proximity to black Africa that gives Botswana some flexibility in terms of possible trade routes and access to the rest of Africa helps to turn the attention of Botswana away from Swaziland and Lesotho. This contact also puts strains on the government to support the various African exile movements that would like to use Botswana as a staging area and sanctuary in their struggle to liberate Southwest Africa (Namibia) and South Africa. This problem, coupled with increasing numbers of refugees from Angola, has placed severe burdens on the government. At the same

24. Sir Seretse Khama, "Outlook for Botswana," *Journal of Modern African Studies* 8, no. 1 (April 1970): 123–128.

25. Richard Dale, "Botswana," *Southern Africa in Perspective* (New York: Free Press, 1972) and his earlier, *Botswana and Its Southern Neighbor: The Patterns of Linkage and the Options in Statecraft* (Athens: Ohio University Center for International Studies, 1970); Edwin S. Munger, *Bechuanaland: Pan-African Outpost or Bantu Homeland?* (London: Oxford University Press, 1965); W. A. J. Macartney, "Botswana Goes to the Polls," *Africa Report* 14, no. 8 (December 1969): 28–30; Stevens, *Lesotho, Botswana, and Swaziland,* pp. 112–172; and Halpern, *South Africa's Hostages,* pp. 261–332. Other, more historical works include A. Sillery, *The Bechuanaland Protectorate* (London and New York: Oxford University Press, 1952); Tshedkedi Khama, *Bechuanaland and South Africa* (London: Africa Bureau, 1955); and idem, *Bechuanaland: A General Survey* (Johannesburg: Institute of Race Relations, 1957). An insightful novel about present-day life in Botswana is Bessie Head's *When Rainclouds Gather* (New York: Simon and Schuster, 1969).

time, although the government of Botswana received American aid for the building of an all-weather road from Nata to Kazungula on the Zambian border, it continues to depend overwhelmingly on transportation routes through South Africa and Rhodesia. Interestingly enough, in terms of future cooperation, the recent Swazi-Zambian trade agreements (which call for the export of cattle products by Swaziland) indicate that Swaziland and Botswana may be moving into direct economic competition with one another.

Thus, if one scans the current levels of interaction among Botswana, Lesotho, and Swaziland, one must conclude that, while the three territories share something of a common heritage and a current state of economic and military vulnerability, each has a relatively minor impact on the national behavior of the others.

If Lesotho and Botswana have only marginal impact on the national life of Swaziland, the Portuguese-controlled territory of Mozambique grows in importance yearly. This was not always the case. Until the 1960s, there was very little interaction between Swaziland and Mozambique. Mozambique was generally in the same relation to Swaziland as Swaziland was to South Africa: more backward economically and less politically aware. With the building of the Swaziland railroad, however, Mozambique became of enormous import, for the port of Lourenço Marques became the central shipping point for most Swaziland exports, most importantly iron ore, sugar, and forestry products. The railroad does enable the Swazis to bargain with the South Africans, but its location also makes Swaziland vulnerable to Portuguese pressure in time of national crisis and further dampens Swazi enthusiasm for the African nationalist movements in the Portuguese-controlled territories.

Although there is currently little trade between the two countries, it is increasing. Swazi manufactures were well represented at the last two trade fairs in Lourenço Marques, and the Portuguese firm of Matola Cement recently established a $700,000 plant at Matsapa. There is also growing cooperation with regard to the use of water resources. Many of the major rivers flowing through Swaziland (such as the Komati, Lomati,

Little, and Great Usutu) originate in South Africa and terminate in Mozambique. Since 1970, there have been a number of discussions among the governments of the three territories to work out joint policies for water usage. Because of the importance of irrigation to the Swazi economy and the implications of that irrigation for Mozambique, levels of governmental interaction should increase markedly over the next few years. In addition, 13 percent of the work force in Swaziland is foreign born and the majority is from southern Mozambique.[26] While most Mozambiqueans work on the sugar plantations and in the mills where there has been little talk of "localization," Portugal believes that employment opportunities in Swaziland are of vital importance for the economic future of its territory. Reflecting the importance of Swaziland, Portugal was the first country outside of Great Britain to establish a resident ambassador in Mbabane.

Future developments in Mozambique could have the most serious implications for Swaziland. The Portuguese presence does not provide the Swazis with many political options with regard to South Africa; if an African government were to come to power in Mozambique, however, Swaziland would be able, perhaps even forced, to change its policy which currently supports the status quo. The Swazi have been insulated from many of the pressures that have been exerted on such states as Zambia and Tanzania to support the liberation of Southern Africa. The arc of white-controlled states surrounding Swaziland has provided a substantial buffer against the full force of the winds of change. Were that situation to change, particularly if African majority rule were attained in Mozambique, Swaziland would be forced to reassess its position and might even be caught in the middle of a struggle for South Africa. This prospect is not particularly appealing to the Swazis, who see it as jeopardizing their economic development and political tranquility. There is, hence, very little enthusiasm within the present Swazi government for an African take-over of Mozambique.

26. Government of Swaziland, *Swaziland, 1969* (Mbabane: Government Printer, 1970), p. 11.

If Mozambique and South Africa have continued to grow in importance for the Swazi, Great Britain's prominence has declined since independence. For nearly a century, Great Britain was the most important restraining influence on South Africa and, in the postwar era, the single most important political and economic force on the Swazi scene. This situation has changed a good deal since the middle 1960s, and it would not be going too far to say that this decline dates from the declaration of independence by the breakaway regime in Rhodesia in November 1965. British unwillingness or inability to defeat the government of Ian Smith signaled an important turning point; Great Britain has steadily disengaged itself from the Southern African context from that time onward. This withdrawal has been most pronounced in the military field. When the first British troops were flown into Swaziland during 1963, Britain seemed to be indicating that it felt its continued presence in the area was of importance; and four separate regiments were rotated to enable Britain to keep a ready reserve on hand. When these troops were suddenly withdrawn in November 1966, and other British units were later pulled out of Botswana, the Swazis were quick to recognize that this signaled the end of an era. With a small police force of 650 men and no army, the Swazis realized that they could not guarantee their territorial integrity by military means and began readjusting their policy accordingly.

In the economic sphere as well, Great Britain has been phasing down its year-by-year commitments to Swaziland. With the new customs agreements, Britain no longer contributes $3 to $4 million worth of budgetary assistance and has scaled down its current development aid to $14 million, to be spread over the next three years. Also, Great Britain has been the primary customer for Swazi forest products and sugar; but with its application for membership in the European Economic Community, this market is no longer assured. Since Great Britain has traditionally purchased Swazi sugar at prices well above the world market, a drastic dislocation of that industry may result as the Swazis seek alternative markets for their annual production of over 160,000 short tons of sugar. It is possible that special arrangements will be made when Britain enters the Common Market. In any case, Great Britain's financial support of Swaziland is clearly declining.

This is not to say that Great Britain is withdrawing entirely from Swaziland affairs. Her Majesty's government will undoubtedly continue its high commissioner in Swaziland and seek to maintain British investment opportunities; but over the longer term, Great Britain lacks the inclination to support the economic development of the country and a continuing process of disengagement can be anticipated.

In the face of these realities, Swaziland is attempting to widen its contacts with two groups of states—with the industrialized countries of Western Europe and Japan, and with the rest of black Africa. Swaziland has no fewer than five of its seven diplomatic missions oriented toward non-African countries. The country is represented in the United States, Great Britain, Canada, France, and Belgium; while Great Britain, the United States, Japan, Portugal, Taiwan, Austria, Switzerland, Sweden, and Iran have diplomatic representation in Mbabane. The other two Swazi missions, at the United Nations and in Kenya, are directly concerned with relations with the states north of the Zambezi. The present government of Swaziland has indicated its eagerness for foreign investment, aid, and trade; and since independence, these types of transactions have grown considerably in volume and scope. Japan, for example, plays a very important economic role at the present time, taking the bulk of the nation's iron ore. In 1970 Japanese steel producers agreed to purchase an additional 7.5 million tons of ore, thereby extending the life of the mine to 1978 at the very least. Negotiations are also under way with regard to Japanese development of Swaziland's considerable coal resources.

The United States has a small but growing presence in Swaziland and could, over time, loom large in the economic picture. Presently, the United States has a chargé d'affaires in Mbabane and a forty-five-member Peace Corps contingent. In 1971 it moved the Office of the Southern African Regional Activities Coordination (OSARAC) from Zambia to Mbabane. During 1969 the United States delivered over $350,000 worth of surplus food to mitigate the effects of a prolonged drought in the low veld and continues to provide small amounts of technical assistance and training opportunities. The United States presence is likely to grow as more American firms invest in Swaziland (many of them to take advantage of the lucrative South African market without suffering the attention of anti-apartheid groups in the United States) and because of the American government's interest in supporting the three former High Commission Territories as multiracial models: "They are seeking to create multiracial societies free of the predominant influence of the minority-dominated states adjoining and surrounding them. They cannot exist without a realistic relationship with their neighbors. At the same time it is in the interest of all those who wish to see the states develop and prosper to provide alternative sources of assistance and means of access to these states." [27] In this context, it seems likely that Swaziland will receive increasing amounts of private venture capital from the United States and will be the recipient of stepped-up foreign aid. For example, the United States could be a significant factor in maintaining the Swazi sugar industry if it would increase the Swazi yearly quota which currently runs under 10,000 tons. The United States will also undoubtedly augment the technical assistance already provided by West Germany, Sweden, and Taiwan. West German firms have also agreed to purchase 63,000 tons of iron ore.

Other countries that have shown increased interest in Swaziland are Denmark, South Korea, and Israel. Holiday Inns International recently opened a new complex in connection with a local firm, Royal Swazispa. In addition to these sources, Swaziland is increasing its contacts with and generating support from major international organizations. In 1969 the country joined the International Monetary Fund (and received a drawing quota of $4.3 million), the International Bank for Reconstruction and Development, the International Finance Corporation, and the International Development Association. In addition, Swaziland has been a major bene-

27. United States Department of State, *United States and Africa in the 1970s* (Washington: Government Printer, 1970), p. 9.

ficiary of the United Nations Development Program, gathering over $2 million in aid by 1970, including a grant of nearly $900,000 for the stimulation of local industries and handicraft concerns throughout the country. Additional United Nations funds have gone to underwrite a survey of Swaziland's water facilities and for a geographical and geochemical overview of the entire country. In attempting to compensate for the reduced rates of Commonwealth Development Corporation support, the government of Swaziland has indeed sought to tap a wide variety of sources.

Since independence, Swaziland has also sought to break out of its isolation in Southern Africa by increasing its contacts with black Africa. We have already examined the Imbokodvo rapprochement with Africa north of the Zambezi which began in 1965. With independence, Swaziland was accepted into the Organization of African Unity, and the country's international standing seems to have benefited from adoption by the East and Central African States of the Lusaka Manifesto in April 1969. While affirming the need for African majority rule in Southern Africa and the end to racism, the signatures indicated that they preferred peaceful change and recognized the dilemma of those African states caught up in the texture of Southern Africa.[28] Since then, overt criticism of Swaziland, Lesotho, and Botswana on the part of other African nations has been greatly reduced. The Swazis have also made a real effort to adopt some of the international aspects of Pan-Africanism and to attack those white minority governments with which Swaziland has no contacts. For example, Prince Makhosini gave a major speech at the Commonwealth conference during January 1969 in which he lashed out at the "Rhodesian sellout." [29] The speech received a good deal of publicity in both Swaziland and East Africa and may well have been timed to precede Swaziland's announcement that it wished to join the East African Common Market.

28. Delegates of the East and Central African States, *The Lusaka Manifesto on Southern Africa* (Dar es Salaam: Government Printer 1969). The manifesto was signed by the representatives of Tanzania, Uganda, Zambia, Somalia, Rwanda, Ethiopia, the Sudan, both Congos, Chad, the Central African Republic, and Burundi.

29. *Times of Swaziland* 67, no. 3 (January 17, 1969): 1, 12.

Following up on this initiative, Swaziland sent delegations to Kenya, Uganda, Tanzania, Malawi, and Zambia, eventually signing trade agreements with all five. Those with Malawi, Kenya, and Zambia turned out to be the most substantial. Malawi agreed to take Swazi sugar and wood pulp in exchange for tea. Kenya sought citrus and coal and in return agreed to send maize, tea, coffee, and soda ash. Kenya in particular asked for, and apparently received, assurances that items of South African origin would not be reexported to Kenya. Of the three agreements, that with Zambia might well have the greatest potential for Swaziland. If trade could develop between the two countries, it would give Swaziland access to a lucrative market at the very time when the leaders of Zambia are vigorously looking for alternative sources to South Africa and Rhodesia. With the Unilateral Declaration of Independence by Rhodesia in 1965, Zambia sought to reorient its trade away from Rhodesia. In order to do so without a drastic increase in the cost of living, it was forced to replace Rhodesian goods with those of South Africa. This has increasingly become a political liability and source of embarrassment to the government of President Kenneth Kaunda. With the completion of the Tanzania-Zambia railroad, Zambia may be able to reorient most of her trade toward East Africa; but in the meantime Swaziland has an excellent opportunity to supply Zambia with meat, citrus fruit, and vegetables.

Thus, in assessing the future of Swaziland we see a stable government—an interesting blend of tradition and political modernity—enjoying widespread support from its population although prodded by a reasonably vibrant opposition. It is a small, weak, economically dependent country which is seeking to the best of its ability to reduce its reliance on any single country or bloc of countries. Swaziland has sought international support for its political independence and economic development, and it has thus far been reasonably successful in both endeavors. Moreover, its relative wealth gives Swaziland an important stake in the status quo in Southern Africa, which, coupled with the traditional orientation of its government, indicates that Swaziland will not challenge the structure of Southern Africa in the foreseeable future. If there is a potentially explosive area in Africa south of the Zambezi, the odds seem overwhelming that it is not in Swaziland.

Bibliography

Articles

Agar-Hamilton, J. A. I. "The South African Protectorates." *Journal of African Society* 29 (1928–29): 12–26.

Apter, David E. "The Role of Traditionalism in the Political Modernization of Ghana and Uganda." *World Politics* 13, no. 4 (1960): 45–68.

Arden-Clarke, Sir Charles. "The Problem of the High Commission Territories." *Optima* 8, no. 4 (December 1958): 163–170.

Ashburner, W. F. "Massive Scheme Brings Fertility to Swaziland." *Farmers Weekly*, no. 103 (May 30, 1962): 18.

Baring, E. "Problems of the High Commission Territories." *International Affairs* 28 (April 1952): 184–189.

Beattie, J. H. M. "Checks on the Abuse of Political Power in Some African States: A Preliminary Framework for Analysis." *Sociologus* 9, no. 2 (1959): 97–115.

Becker, P. L. W. "Untouched by Western Civilization." *Farmers Weekly*, no. 93 (December 11, 1957): 23–25.

Bowman, Larry W. "The Subordinate State System of Southern Africa." *International Studies Quarterly* 12, no. 3 (September 1968): 231–261.

Brooks, Charles. "On the Banks of the Great Usutu River." *Swaziland Recorder*, no. 2 (March–June 1961): 19.

———. "Paramount Chief Speaks of Swaziland's Future." *Swaziland Recorder*, no. 4 (September–December 1961): p. 21.

Butler, P. "Ritual Murder." *Outspan*, no. 51 (April 4, 1952): 38–41.

Carter, Gwendolen M. "Sacred Fertility Festival." *Africa Special Report* 2, no. 4 (April 1957): 5.

Carter, W. M. "Colonial Development Corporation's Swaziland Investment." *Swaziland Recorder*, no. 7 (July–September 1962): 138.

Clark, W. M. "Views on the Constitution of Swaziland." *Swaziland Recorder*, no. 14 (March–June 1964): 11–19.

———. "Problems of the Protectorates." *Spectator* 183 (November 25, 1949): 731.

Clark, W. M. "Marshall Clark Looks at Swaziland's Economic Future." *Swaziland Recorder,* no. 9 (January–March 1963): 15–17.

———. "Swazi Economy." *South Africa Financial Mail,* July 17, 1964, pp. 140–143.

———. "Swaziland Mineral Deposits." *South African Mine Engineers Journal,* no. 74 (November 15, 1963): 323.

———. "Swaziland Split Personality." *South African Financial Mail,* no. 10 (November 1, 1963): 466–468.

———. "United Kingdom Government Prepares Final Analysis of Necessities." *Swaziland Recorder,* no. 10 (March–June 1963): 11–19.

Coates, Austin. "Angola and Mozambique." *Swaziland Recorder,* no. 18 (March–June 1965): 8.

Cockram, Ben. "The Protectorates: An International Problem." *Optima* 13, no. 4 (December 1963): 21, 177–183.

Cowin, K. "Know Your District." *Farmers Weekly,* no. 90 (December 7, 1955): 23–25.

Daniel, J. B. McI. "Swaziland: Some Problems of an African Rural Economy in a Developing Country." *South African Geographical Journal* 48 (December 1966): 90–100.

Davidson, Basil. "Country of King Sobhuza." *New Statesman* 46 (September 19, 1953): 308; (October 3, 1953): 367–368.

Day, John. "Southern Rhodesian African Nationalists and the 1961 Constitution." *Journal of Modern African Studies* 7, no. 2 (1969): 221–477.

Doveton, D. M. "Economic Geography of Swaziland." *Geographical Journal* 88 (October 1936): 322–331.

Dumbrell, H. J. E. "Pyre Burning in Swaziland." *African Study* 11 (1952): 109–119.

Eisenstadt, S. N. "Primitive Political Systems: A Preliminary Comparative Analysis." *American Anthropologist* 61 (1959): 200–220.

Fair, T. J. D., and Green, L. P. "Preparing for Swaziland's Future Economic Growth." *Optima* 10, no. 4 (December 1960): 194–206.

Fife, D. "Tour of Swaziland." *Lantern* 2 (October 1952): 157–159.

Fitzgerald, R. C. "South Africa and the High Commission Territories." *World Affairs* 4, no. 3 (July 1950): 306–320.

Gluckman, Max. "The Kingdom of the Zulu of South Africa." In M. Fortes and E. E. Evans-Pritchard (eds.), *African Political Systems* (London: Oxford University Press, 1940), pp. 25–55.

Gordon, W. R. "Swaziland." *Contemporary* 177 (February 1950): 91–94.

Gray, Alan. "Three 'Islands' in South Africa." *New Commonwealth,* July 1961.

Gross, Ernst A. "The Coalescing Problem of Southern Africa." *Foreign Affairs* 46, no. 4 (July 1968): 743–757.

Gross, S. I. "Basutoland, Bechuanaland Protectorate, Swaziland." *Board of Trade Journal* 183 (September 28, 1962): 641–646.

Halpern, J. "South Africa: Enclaves of Trouble." *Nation* 197 (July 27, 1963).

Hawkins, L. A. W. "Excellent Progress with Railway." *Swaziland Recorder,* no. 13 (January–March 1964): 9–13.

———. "Important Ore Line Will Be Ready for Traffic." *Railway Engineering* 8 (1964): 26–27.

———. "Rich Iron Ore Deposits Give Swaziland Its Long-Awaited Railroad." *Optima* 14, no. 2 (June 1964): 84–87.

———. "Swaziland and Its Ocean Outlet." *African Roads* 21, no. 4 (April 1964): 12–13.

———. "Planning Standardization and Mechanization." *South African Mining Engineering Journal* 75 (November 13, 1964): 1366–1368.

Herd, Norman. "Swaziland's Mineral Projects Must Be Regarded as Bright." *South African Mining Engineering Journal* 74 (February 8, 1963): 307–308.

———. "Maize for Swazi Famine Relief." *Swaziland Recorder,* no. 6 (March–June 1962): 33.

———. "Modern Techniques Revive Hope in New Gold Deposits." *Swaziland Recorder,* no. 10 (March–June 1963): 15–19.

———. "Public Discussion of New Constitution." *Swaziland Recorder,* no. 5 (January–March 1962): 15–16.

———. "Swaziland's Advance." *Swaziland Recorder,* no. 8 (September–December 1962): 19–21.

———. "Green Light on the Swaziland Railroad." *Industrial Review of Africa* 12, no. 10 (May 1961): 8.

———. "Track Beds Being Prepared." *Swaziland Recorder,* no. 12 (September–December 1963): 23–25.

———. "Carl Todd Looks at Swaziland." *Swaziland Recorder,* no. 16 (September–December 1964): 11–15.

———. "Foreign Trade of the Union of South Africa (including South West Africa, Basutoland, Swaziland, and the Bechuanaland Protectorate." *Trade Review* 4 (March 1960): 11.

———. "This Is Swaziland." *Swaziland Recorder,* no. 1 (January–March 1961): 7–10.

Hodgson, M. L. "Britain as Trustee in Southern Africa." *Political Quarterly* 3 (July 1932): 398–408.

Holloway, J. E. "South Africa Remains a Sound Investment Field." *Optima* 11, no. 2 (September 1961): 113–115.

Houlton, John. "The High Commission Territories in South Africa." *Geographical Magazine* 26 (August 1953): 175–181.

Howe, Russell Warren. "War in Southern Africa." *Foreign Affairs* 48, no. 1 (October 1969): 150–165.

Hughes, A. J. B. "Some Swazi Views on Land Tenure." *Africa: Journal of the International Institute* 32, no. 3 (July 1962): 253–278.

Hughes, A. J. B. "Reflections on Traditional and Individual Land Tenure in Swaziland." *Journal of Local Administration Overseas* 3, no. 1 (January 1964): 3–13.

Hunter, D. R. "Geology of Swaziland." *Geology Society of South Africa* 60 (1957): 85–125.

Khale, J. E. "Swazis on the Move." *Our Africa* 2 (July 1960): 5–7.

Khama, Sir Seretse. "Outlook for Botswana." *Journal of Modern African Studies* 8, no. 1 (April 1970): 123–128.

Kruger, C. M. "Contract to Supply Rails." *Swaziland Recorder*, no. 6 (March–June 1962): 27.

Kuper, Hilda. "The Swazi of Swaziland." In J. L. Gibbs (ed.), *Peoples of Africa* (New York: Holt, Rinehart, and Winston, 1965), pp. 479–512.

———. "The Development of the Military Organization of Swaziland." *Africa* 10 (1937): 55–74, 176–205.

———. "The Swazi." in Daryll Forde (ed.), *Ethnographic Survey of Southern Africa* (London: International African Institute, 1952).

———. "Kinship Among the Swazi." In A. R. Radcliffe-Brown and Daryll Forde (eds.), *African Systems of Kinship and Marriage* (London: Oxford University Press, 1950), pp. 86–110.

———. "A Ritual of Kingship Among the Swazi." *Africa* (London) 14, no. 5 (January 1944): 230–257.

Lloyd, Peter C. "Traditional Rulers." In James S. Coleman and Carl G. Rosberg, Jr. (eds.), *Political Parties and National Integration in Tropical Africa* (Berkeley and Los Angeles: University of California Press, 1966), pp. 382–412.

Macartney, W. A. J. "Botswana Goes to the Polls." *Africa Report* 14, no. 8 (December 1969): 28–30.

Martin, A. "Constitutional Aftermath." *Swaziland Recorder*, no. 16 (September–December 1964): 29–30.

Maud, Sir John. "The Challenge of the High Commission Territories." *African Affairs* 63 (April 1964): 94–103.

———. "My Hopes for Swaziland." *Swaziland Recorder*, no. 10 (March–June 1963): 11–13.

Miller, I. "Partnership with Private Enterprise." *Swaziland Recorder*, no. 14 (March–June 1964): 23–25.

Miller, Norman N. "The Political Survival of Traditional Leadership." *Journal of Modern African Studies* 6, no. 2 (1968): 183–198.

———. "The Rural African Party: Political Participation in Tanzania." *American Political Science Review* 64, no. 2 (June 1970): 548–571.

Mohlomi, G. "Royal Swazi Wedding." *Zonk* 15 (September 1963): 15–17.

———. "Swaziland: Panic or Progress." *South African Financial Mail* 8 (March 1963): 11–13.

Mollatt, E. B. "Chief Knew His Onions." *Outspan* 15 (July 1, 1955): 34–35.

————. "Swaziland's Development." *South African Mining Engineering Journal* 70 (March 20, 1954): 589–591.

————. "Swaziland Means Business." *Outspan* 15 (June 1955): 23–25.

Moses, Macdonald. "Havelock Mine Report: Coming Clash in Swaziland." *Newscheck* (Johannesburg), October 11, 1963, p. 24.

Ngwane National Liberatory Congress, "White Settler's Conspiracy Exposed." Press release, November 12, 1965.

Niven, D. J. "Nonracial State Is Theme of Planners." *Swaziland Recorder,* no. 3 (July–September 1961): 25.

Pim, Sir Alan W. "Question of the South African Protectorates." *International Affairs* 13, no. 3 (September 1934): 668–688.

Pirie, J. H. H. "Swaziland Postal History and Stamps." *South African Philatelist* 29 (August 1953): 24–26.

Potholm, C. P. "The Protectorates, the O.A.U., and South Africa." *International Journal* 22, no. 1 (winter 1966–67): 68–72.

————. "Changing Political Configurations in Swaziland." *Journal of Modern African Studies* 4, no. 3 (November 1966): 313–322.

————. "Swaziland in Transition of Independence." *Africa Report* 12, no. 6 (June 1967): 49–54.

Pott, D. "Swaziland: A General Survey." *Race Relations* 18 (1951): 125–265.

Reilly, T. E. "Native Reserve in Swaziland." *African Wild Life* 14 (June 1960): 113–115.

————. "Protectorate with a Future." *South African Financial Mail* 7 (November 2, 1962): 73–75.

————. "Swaziland's Mine Railway Project." *South African Mining Engineering Journal* 72 (September 1961): 685–687.

Robertson, T. C. "Swaziland Magic." *Libertas* 4, no. 12 (November 1944): 18–37.

Robson, Peter. "Economic Integration in Southern Africa." *Journal of Modern African Studies* 5, no. 4 (December 1967): 469–490.

Rose, B. "Swaziland: A Contemporary Survey." *African World,* May, 1965, p. 5.

Rubin, L., and Stevens, R. P. "The High Commission Territories: What Now?" *African Report* 9, no. 4 (April 1964): 9–17.

Skinner, Elliott P. "The 'Paradox' of Rural Leadership: A Comment." *Journal of Modern African Studies* 6, no. 2 (1968): 198–201.

Sklar, Richard L. "Political Science and National Integration." *Journal of Modern African Studies* 5, no. 1 (1967): 1–11.

Smit, P. "Swaziland: Resources and Development." *Swaziland on the Eve of Independence.* Pretoria: Africa Institute of South Africa, 1969, pp. 15–31.

Smit, P., and van der Merwe, E. J. "Economic Co-operation in Southern Africa." *Journal of Geography* (Stellenbosch) 3, no. 3 (September 1968): 279–294.

Smith, D. "Railroad Key to Many New Industries." *Swaziland Recorder,* no. 16 (September–December 1964): 15–19.

Spence, J. E. "The High Commission Territories with Special Reference to Swaziland." In Burton Benedict (ed.), *Problems of Smaller Territories* (London: Athlone Press, 1967), p. 98.

Standard Bank Organization. "Southern African Customs Union." *Standard Bank Review* (London), July 1970, pp. 7–10.

Stevens, R. P. "Southern Africa's Multiracial University." *African Report* 9, no. 3 (March 1964): 16–18.

———. "Swaziland: A Constitution Imposed." *African Report,* April 1964.

———. "Swaziland Political Development." *Journal of Modern African Studies* 1, no. 3 (September 1963): 327–350.

Suret-Canale, Jean. "The End of Chieftaincy in Guinea." *Journal of African History* 7, no. 3 (1966): 459–493.

Thain, G. M. "Focus on Mineral Wealth in Recent Geographical Surveys." *Swaziland Recorder,* no. 6 (March–June 1962): 31.

———. "Kaolin." *Swaziland Recorder,* no. 7 (July–September 1962): 19.

———. "Swaziland Minerals." *Swaziland Recorder,* no. 18 (March–June 1965): 21.

———. "Swaziland Has Scope for a Small Mines Industry." *Swaziland Recorder,* no. 5 (January–March 1962): 21.

———. "Swaziland Railroad." *Swaziland Recorder,* no. 2 (March–June 1961): 13.

Thompson, A. C. "The Republic and the High Commission Territories." *Swaziland Recorder,* no. 1 (January–March 1961): 11.

———. "Swaziland's First Building Society." *Swaziland Recorder,* no. 5 (January–March 1962): 25.

———. "Mhlume." *South African Mining Engineer Journal* 53 (May 1962): 28–29.

———. "Railway Comes to Swaziland." *Swaziland Recorder,* no. 3 (July–September 1961): 8–9.

———. "Tracking the Railroad." *Swaziland Recorder,* no. 5 (January–March 1962): 19.

Thompson, Leonard. "The Zulu Kingdom." In Monica Wilson and Leonard Thompson (eds.), *The Oxford History of South Africa* (London: Oxford University Press, 1969), 1:336–364.

Twala, R. G. "Beads as Regulating the Social Life of the Zulu and the Swazi." *African Studies* 10 (1951): 113–123.

———. "Umhlanga." *African Studies* 11 (1952): 93–104.

Wallerstein, Immanuel M. "Ethnicity and National Integration in West Africa." *Cahiers d'Etudes Africaines* 3, no. 1 (October 1960): 129–139.

Warden, W. "New Ore Line." *Railway Engineering* 8 (November–December 1964): 23–57.

———. "Steel for the Swaziland Railroad." *Iscar News* 29 (July 1964): 6–10.

Watt, C. J. "Swaziland." *Travel in Africa* 1 (March 1952): 25–26.

———. "Swaziland National Festival." *African World,* December 1952, pp. 11–12.

———. "Conditions in Swaziland." *Farmer's Weekly* 79 (August 2, 1950): 29–31.

Weisfelder, Richard. "Power Struggle in Lesotho." *Africa Report* 12, no. 1 (January 1967): 5–13.

Welch, Claude E., Jr. "Constitutional Confusion in Swaziland." *Africa Report* 8, no. 45 (April 1963): 7–9.

Whitaker, C. S. "A Dysrhythmic Process of Political Change." *World Politics* 19, no. 2 (1967): 190–217.

Whithe, E. "Last Steps Towards Independence." *African Affairs* 64, no. 257 (October 1965): 261–270.

Young, B. S. "High Commission Territories of Southern Africa." *Focus* 14 (December 1963): 1–6.

Zwane, Timothy. "The Struggle for Power in Swaziland." *Africa Today* 11 (May 1964): 4–6.

Books, Pamphlets, and Documents

Abercrombie, H. R. *Africa's Peril.* London: Simpkin Marshall, 1938.

Agar-Hamilton, J. A. I. *The Native Policy of the Voortrekkers.* Cape Town: Maskew Miller, 1928.

Allighan, Garry. *Curtain-up on South Africa.* London and New York: Boardman, 1960.

Andrews, H. T. (ed.). *South Africa in the Sixties.* Cape Town: South African Foundation, 1965.

Apter, David E. *The Political Kingdom in Uganda.* Princeton: Princeton University Press, 1967; rev. ed.

Ardizzone, M. *The Mistaken Land.* London: Falcon Press, 1951.

Arnheim, J. W. *Swaziland: A Bibliography.* Cape Town: School of Librarianship, 1950; reprinted, 1963.

Ashton, E. *The Basuto.* London: Oxford University Press, 1962.

Austin, Dennis. *Britain and South Africa.* London: Oxford University Press, 1966.

Ballinger, W. G. *Race and Economics in South Africa.* London: Hogarth Press, 1934.

Barber, James. *Rhodesia: The Road to Rebellion.* London: Oxford University Press, 1967.

Barclays Bank. *Basutoland, Bechuanaland, and Swaziland.* London: Barclays Bank D.C.O., 1962.

Barker, Dudley. *Swaziland.* London: Her Majesty's Stationery Office, 1965.

Barnes, Leonard. *The New Boer War.* London: Hogarth Press, 1932.

Batson, E. *Swaziland Agricultural Survey.* Cape Town: School of Social Studies, University of Cape Town, 1953.

Becker, Peter. *Rule of Fear: The Life and Times of Dingane, King of the Zulu.* London: Longmans, 1964.

Bell, F. W. *The South African Conspiracy.* London: Heinemann, 1900.

Benson, Mary. *The African Patriots: The Story of the African National Congress.* London: Faber and Faber, 1963; New York: Atheneum, 1964.

Best, Alan C. *The Swaziland Railway.* East Lansing: Michigan State University, 1966.

Bigelow, P. *White Man's Africa.* New York and London: Harper and Brothers, 1899.

Bixler, R. W. *Anglo-German Imperialism in South Africa.* Baltimore: Warwick and York, 1932.

Black, M. R. *No Room for Tourists.* London: Secker and Warburg, 1965.

Blackwell, Leslie. *This Is South Africa.* Pietermaritzburg: Shuter and Shuter, 1947.

Brady, A. *Democracy in the Dominions.* Toronto: University of Toronto Press, 1947.

Brand, R. H. *The Union of South Africa.* Oxford: Clarendon Press, 1909.

British Information Service. *The High Commission Territories.* London: Central Office of Information, 1963.

————. *Apartheid: Challenge to British Policy.* London: Her Majesty's Stationery Office, 1964.

Brookes, Edgar H. *Apartheid: A Documentary Study of Modern South Africa.* London: Routledge & Kegan Paul, 1968.

————. *The City of God and the City of Man in Africa.* Lexington: University of Kentucky Press, 1964.

————. *South Africa in a Changing World.* Cape Town: Oxford University Press, 1953.

Bryant, A. T. *Olden Times in Zululand and Natal.* London: Longmans, Green, 1929.

Bryce, J. B. *Impressions of South Africa.* New York: Century, 1900.

Buchan, John. *The African Colony.* Edinburgh and London: Blackwood, 1903.

Bulpin, T. V. *Storm over the Transvaal.* Cape Town: Standard Press, 1955.

————. *The White Whirlwind.* Johannesburg: H. F. G. Witherby, 1938.

Bunting, B. P. *The Rise of the South African Reich.* Harmondsworth, Middlesex: Penguin, 1964.

Callan, E. *Albert John Luthuli and the South African Race Conflict*. Kalamazoo: Western Michigan University Press, 1962.

Cana, F. R. *South Africa from the Great Trek to the Union*. London: Chapman & Hall, 1909.

Carter, Gwendolen M. (ed.). *Five African States*. Ithaca: Cornell University Press, 1963.

———. *The Politics of Inequality*. New York: Praeger, 1958.

———. *South Africa*. New York: Foreign Policy Association, 1955.

Carter, Gwendolen M.; Karis, Thomas; and Stultz, Newell M. *South Africa's Transkei: The Politics of Domestic Colonialism*. Evanston: Northwestern University Press, 1967.

Cecil, Evelyn. *On the Eve of the War*. London: Murray, 1900.

Cervenka, Zdenek. *The Organization of African Unity and Its Charter*. New York: Praeger, 1968.

Churchill, R. *White Man's God*. New York: Morrow, 1962.

Cockram, Ben. *Problems of Southern Africa*. Johannesburg: South African Institute of International Affairs, 1963.

Cohen, Ronald, and Middleton, John (eds.). *From Tribe to Nation in Africa*. Scranton, Penn.: Chandler, 1970).

Cole, E. *House of Bondage*. New York: Random House, 1967.

Cowen, D. V. *Report on Constitutional Reform*. Cape Town: Lincey and Watson, 1961.

———. *The Foundations of Freedom*. Cape Town and New York: Oxford University Press, 1961.

Creswicke, Louis. *South Africa and the Transvaal*. Edinburgh: T. C. and E. C. Jack, 1900.

Dale, Richard. *Botswana and Its Southern Neighbor: The Patterns of Linkage and the Options in Statecraft*. Athens: Ohio University Center for International Studies, 1970.

Daniel, J. B. McI. *The Geography of the Rural Economy of Swaziland*. Durban: Institute for Social Research, University of Natal, 1962.

Davenport, T. R. H. *The Africaner Bond*. Cape Town: Oxford University Press, 1966.

Davies, D. N., and Urie, J. G. *The Bomvu Ridge Harmatite Deposits*. Mbabane: Government Printer, 1956.

Davis, Alexander. *Umbandine*. London: Unwin, 1898.

Davis, Gordon, and Melunsky, L. *Urban Native Law*. Port Elizabeth: Grotius, 1959.

Davis, John A., and Baker, James K. (eds.). *Southern Africa in Transition*. New York: Praeger, 1966.

Dawson, W. H. *South Africa: Peoples, Places, and Problems*. New York: Longmans, Green, 1925.

De Beer, Z. J. *Multi-racial South Africa*. London: Oxford University Press, 1961.

de Blij, Harm I. *A Geography of Southern Africa*. Chicago: Rand McNally, 1964.

De Kiewiet, C. W. *Anatomy of South African Misery*. London: Oxford University Press, 1956.

———. *The Imperial Factor in South Africa*. Cambridge: University Press, 1937.

———. *A History of South Africa*. London: Oxford University Press, 1957.

De Kock, Victor. *Those in Bondage*. London: Allen and Unwin, 1950.

Delegates of East and Central African States. *The Lusaka Manifesto on Southern Africa*. Dar es Salaam: Government Printer, 1969.

Doveton, Dorothy. *The Human Geography of Swaziland*. London: George Philip and Son, 1937.

Doxey, G. V. *The High Commission Territories and the Republic of South Africa*. London: Oxford University Press, 1963.

———. *The Industrial Colour Bar in South Africa*. Cape Town and New York: Oxford University Press, 1961.

Du Preez, A. B. *Inside the South African Crucible*. Kaapstad, South Africa: H.A.U.M., 1959.

Dundas, Sir Charles, and Ashton, Dr. Hugh. *Problem Territories of Southern Africa*. Johannesburg: South African Institute of International Affairs, 1952.

Edwards, Isobel. *Protectorates or Native Reserves?* London: African Bureau, 1956.

Engelbrecht, J. A. *Swazi Texts with Notes*. Cape Town: Nasionale Pers, 1930.

European Advisory Council. "Minutes of the Reconstituted European Advisory Council." Mimeographed by the government secretary, Mbabane, 1949–1950, 1950–1953, 1954–1955, 1956, 1957, 1958, 1959, 1960, 1961, 1962, 1963, 1964.

Evans, I. L. *Native Policy in Southern Africa*. Cambridge: Cambridge University Press, 1934.

Fair, T. J. D., and Green, L. P. *Development in Africa*. Johannesburg: University of Witwatersrand Press, 1962.

Fair, T. J. D.; Murdoch, G.; and Jones, H. M. *Development in Swaziland*. Johannesburg: University of Witwatersrand Press, 1969.

Farrelly, M. J. *The Settlement After the War in South Africa*. New York: Macmillan, 1900.

Feit, Edward. *South Africa: The Dynamics of the African National Congress*. London: Oxford University Press, 1962.

———. *African Opposition in South Africa*. Stanford: Hoover Institute, 1967.

Filmer, Harry, and Jameson, Patricia. *Usutu*. Johannesburg: Central News Agency, 1960.

Forbes, David. *My Life in South Africa*. London: Witherby, 1938.

Fremantle, H. E. S. *The New Nation*. London: J. Ouseley, 1909.

Gaiger, Sidney. Campaign handout. Mimeographed, n.p., 1964.

Galbraith, John S. *Reluctant Empire: British Policy on the South African Frontier, 1834–1854*. Berkeley and Los Angeles: University of California Press, 1963.

Garson, Noel. *The Swaziland Question and the Road to Sea, 1887–1895*. Johannesburg: University of Witwatersrand Press, 1957.

Giniewski, P. *Bantustans: A Trek Towards the Future*. Cape Town: Human and Rousseau, 1961.

Gluckman, Max. *Rituals of Rebellion*. Manchester: Manchester University Press, 1952.

——. *Politics, Law, and Ritual in Tribal Societies*. Chicago: Aldine, 1965.

Great Britain, Government of. *Basutoland, the Bechuanaland Protectorate, and Swaziland: History of Discussions with the Union of South Africa, 1909–1939*. London: His Majesty's Stationery Office, 1952.

——. British Information Service. *Apartheid: Challenge to British Policy*. London: Her Majesty's Stationery Office, 1964.

——. *Cmnd. No. 2052*. London: Her Majesty's Stationery Office, 1963.

——. *Cmnd. No. 3119*. London: Her Majesty's Stationery Office, 1966.

——. *Cmnd. No. 4114*. London: His Majesty's Stationery Office, 1932.

——. *Cmnd. No. 5089*. London: Her Majesty's Stationery Office, 1887.

——. *Cmnd. No. 6200*. London: Her Majesty's Stationery Office, 1890.

——. *Cmnd. No. 6201*. London: Her Majesty's Stationery Office, 1890.

——. *Cmnd. No. 7212*. London: Her Majesty's Stationery Office, 1893.

——. *Cmnd. No. 7611*. London: Her Majesty's Stationery Office, 1895.

——. *Census of Swaziland, 1956*. Mbabane: Government Printer, 1958.

——. Commonwealth Relations Office. *Batsutoland, Bechuanaland Protectorate, and Swaziland: Report of an Economic Survey Mission*. London: Her Majesty's Stationery Office, 1960.

——. *Commercial Agreement Between the High Commissioner for South Africa and the Governor General of Mozambique Regulating the Commercial Relations Between Swaziland, Basutoland, and the Bechuanaland Protectorate and the Portuguese Colony of Mozambique*. London: His Majesty's Stationery Office, 1930.

——. "Minutes of the Swaziland Constitutional Conference, January 28–February 12, 1963." Mimeographed, London, 1963.

——. *Notes Exchanged Between His Majesty's Government and*

the Government of Portugal for the Settlement of the Boundary Between Swaziland and the Province of Mozambique. London: His Majesty's Stationery Office, 1938.

———. Colonial Office. *Swaziland.* London: His Majesty's Stationery Office, 1946, 1947, 1948, 1949, 1950, 1951, 1952, 1953.

———. *Swaziland.* London: Her Majesty's Stationery Office, 1954, 1955, 1956, 1957, 1961, 1962, 1963.

———. *Swaziland.* London: Her Majesty's Stationery Office, 1964, 1965, 1966, 1967, 1968.

———. *Statistical Abstract for the British Commonwealth 1936–1945.* London: His Majesty's Stationery Office, 1947.

———. *The Swaziland Order of Council, 1963.* London: Her Majesty's Stationery Office, 1963.

Greaves, Lionel Bruce. *The High Commission Territories.* London: Edinburgh House Press, 1953.

———. *The High Commission Territories.* London: British Information Service, 1963.

Gregory, T. E. *Ernest Oppenheimer and the Economic Development of Southern Africa.* Cape Town: Oxford University Press, 1962.

Griffithes, T. P. *From Brelford Row to Swaziland.* London, 1890.

Hailey, Lord. *Native Administration in the British African Territories.* London: His Majesty's Stationery Office, 1953.

———. *An African Survey.* Oxford: Oxford University Press, 1957.

———. *The Republic of South Africa and the High Commission Territories.* London: Oxford University Press, 1963.

Halpern, Jack. *South Africa's Hostages: Basutoland, Bechuanaland, and Swaziland.* Baltimore: Penguin, 1965.

Hance, William (ed.). *Southern Africa and the United States.* New York: Columbia University Press, 1968.

Hancock. W. K. *A Survey of British Commonwealth Affairs.* London: Oxford University Press, 1963.

Hatch, J. C. *The Dilemma of South Africa.* New York: Roy, 1952.

Head, B. *When Rainclouds Gather.* New York: Simon & Schuster, 1969.

Hendy, H. R. *Swaziland: The Tourist's Paradise.* Durban: John Ramsay, 1953.

Herskovits, Melville J. *The Human Factor in Changing Africa.* New York: Knopf, 1962.

Hill, C. R. *Bantustans: The Fragmentation of South Africa.* London and New York: Oxford University Press, 1964.

Hillegas, Howard. *Oom Paul's People.* New York: Appleton, 1899.

Hodgson, Margaret L. *Indirect Rule in Southern Africa.* Alice, South Africa: Lovedale Press, 1931.

Hofmeyr, Jan H. *South Africa.* New York: McGraw-Hill, 1952.

Holleman, J. F. (ed.). *Experiment in Swaziland.* Durban: University of Natal Press, 1964.

Hooker, LeRoy. *The Africanders*. Chicago and New York: Rand, McNally, 1900.

Horrell, Muriel (compiler). *A Survey of Race Relations in South Africa*. Johannesburg: South African Institute of Race Relations, 1964.

Houlton, John. *Board of Inquiry into the Trade Dispute at Havelock Mine*. Mbabane: Government Printer, 1963.

Hughes, A. J. B. *Swazi Land Tenure*. Natal: Institute for Social Research, University of Natal, 1964.

Huskisson, Yvonne. *A Survey of Musical Practices of a Swazi Tribe*. Pretoria: National Council for Social Research, 1960.

Hyatt, Stanley Portal. *The Northward Trek*. London: Melrose, 1909.

Imbokodvo National Movement. *Imbokodvo Emabalababa Constitution*. Mimeographed, n.p., 1964.

Ireland, Alleyne. *The Anglo-Boer Conflict: Its History and Causes*. London: Sands and Company, 1960.

Jones, H. M. *Report on the 1966 Swaziland Population Census*. Mbabane: Government Printer, 1968.

Jones, Sonja. *A Study of Swazi Nutrition*. Durban: University of Natal Press, 1963.

Joseph, H. *If This Be Treason*. London: Deutsch, 1963.

Karis, T. G. *South Africa: The End Is Not Yet*. New York: Foreign Policy Association, 1966.

Khama, Tshedkedi. *Bechuanaland and South Africa*. London: Africa Bureau, 1955.

Krige, D. T., and Krige, T. D. *The Realm of a Rain King*. London: Oxford University Press, 1947.

Kruger, D. W. (ed.). *South African Parties and Policies*. London: Bowes and Bowes, 1960.

Kuper, Hilda. *A Witch in My Heart*. London: Oxford University Press, 1970.

———. *The Uniform of Color*. Johannesburg: University of Witwatersrand Press, 1947.

———. *The Swazi: A South African Kingdom*. New York: Holt, Rinehart, and Winston, 1963.

———. *Bite of Hunger*. New York: Harcourt, Brace, and World, 1965.

———. *An African Aristocracy: Rank Among the Swazis*. London: Oxford University Press, 1947.

Kuper, Leo. *Passive Resistance in South Africa*. London: Cape, 1956.

Kuper, Leo, and Smith, M. G. (eds.). *Pluralism in Africa*. Berkeley and Los Angeles: University of California Press, 1969.

Labouret, Henri. *Africa Before the White Man*. New York: Walker, 1966.

Langdon, G. *The Basutos*. London: Hutchinson, 1909.

Legum, C. *South Africa: Crisis for the West*. New York: Praeger, 1964.

Leistner, G. M. E. *Economic Structure and Growth*. Pretoria: Africa Institute of South Africa, 1966.

Leistner, G. M. E., and Smit, P. *Swaziland: Resources and Development*. Pretoria: African Institute of South Africa, 1969.

Liversage, Vincent. *Land Tenure in the Colonies*. Cambridge: Cambridge University Press, 1945.

Long, W. H. *Peace and War in the Transvaal*. London: Low, Marston, Searle, and Rivington, 1882.

Luthuli, A. J. *Let My People Go*. New York: McGraw-Hill, 1962.

McClellan, G. S. *South Africa*. New York: Wilson, 1962.

MacMillan, William M. *Bantu, Boer, and Briton*. London: Farber and Farber, 1953.

Mair, Lucy. *Primitive Government*. Baltimore: Penguin, 1962.

Mansergh, Nicholas. *South Africa, 1906–1961: The Price of Magnanimity*. New York: Praeger, 1962.

Manzini Indaba Society. *Progress and Prosperity*. Manzini: Manzini Typing and Duplicating Service, 1962.

Marquand, Leo. *The Peoples and Policies of South Africa*. Cape Town: Clarendon Press, 1961.

Marsis, Johannes S. *The Fall of Kruger's Republic*. Oxford: Clarendon Press, 1961.

Marwick, Brian. *Abantu Bakwa Ngwane*. Cape Town: University of Cape Town Press, 1939.

―――. *The Swazi*. Cambridge: Cambridge University Press, 1940.

Mbeki, Govan. *South Africa: The Peasants' Revolt*. Harmondsworth and Baltimore, Md.: Penguin, 1964.

Mears, Gordon. *Methodism in Swaziland*. Rondebosch: Methodist Missionary Department, 1955.

Miller, Allister. *Mamisa: The Swazi Warrior*. Pietermaritzburg: Shuter and Shuter, 1953.

―――. *The South East Coast of Africa and Its Development*. St. Albans: Cambridge Press, 1923.

―――. *Swaziland*. London: Weightman and Company, 1924.

―――. *Swaziland: The California of South Africa*. Mbabane: The Chamber, 1907.

Millin, S. G. *The People of South Africa*. London: Constable, 1951.

Mitchell, N. P. *Land Problems and Policies in the African Mandates of the British Commonwealth*. Baton Rouge: Louisiana State University Press, 1931.

Mohen, J. T. *The Commonwealth Without South Africa*. Toronto: Canadian Institute of International Affairs, 1961.

Moraes, F. R. *The Importance of Being Black*. New York: Macmillan, 1965.

Morris, Donald R. *The Washing of the Spears*. New York: Simon and Schuster, 1965.

Munger, Edwin S. *Bechuanaland: Pan-African Outpost or Bantu Homeland?* London: Oxford University Press, 1965.

———. *Notes on the Formation of the South African Foreign Policy.* Pasadena: Dahlstrom Castle Press, 1965.

———. *Swaziland: The Tribe and the Country.* American Universities Field Service, August 1962.

Nathan, M. *South Africa from Within.* London: Murray, 1926.

———. *The South African Commonwealth.* Johannesburg: Specialty Press, 1919.

Neame, L. E. *The History of Apartheid.* London: Pall Mall Press, 1962.

Neumark, S. D. *Economic Influences on the South Africa Frontier.* Stanford: Stanford University Press, 1957.

Ngwane National Liberatory Congress. "Constitution." Mimeographed, n.p., n.d.

Nicholls, G. H. *South Africa in My Time.* London: Allen and Unwin, 1961.

Norton, George. *Should South Africa Expand?* London: Union of Democratic Control, 1951.

Nquku, J. J. *Geography of Swaziland.* Bremersdorp, Swaziland: Servite Fathers, 1936.

———. "The Swaziland Progressive Party and the Future of Swaziland." Mimeographed, Mbabane, 1963.

Omer-Cooper, J. D. *The Zulu Aftermath.* Evanston: Northwestern University Press, 1966.

O'Neil, Owen Rowe. *Adventures in Swaziland.* London: Allen and Unwin, 1921.

———. *Adventures in Swaziland: The Adventures of a South African Boer.* New York: Century, 1921.

Orchard, Ronald. *The High Commission Territories of South Africa.* London: World Dominion Press, 1951.

Paton, A. *Hope for South Africa.* London: Pall Mall Press, 1958.

———. *South Africa in Transition.* New York: Scribner, 1956.

———. *South African Tragedy.* New York: Scribner, 1965.

Patterson, S. *The Last Trek.* London: Routledge and Kegan Paul, 1957.

Perham, Margery, and Curtis, Lionel. *The Protectorates of South Africa.* London: Oxford University Press, 1935.

Phillips, N. C. *The Tragedy of Apartheid.* New York: McKay, 1960.

Potholm, C. P., and Dale, R. (eds.). *Southern Africa in Perspective: Essays in Regional Politics* (New York: Free Press, forthcoming).

———. *Four African Political Systems.* Englewood Cliffs: Prentice-Hall, 1970.

Pott, Douglas. *Swaziland: A General Survey.* Johannesburg: South African Institute of Race Relations, 1955.

Pyrah, G. B. *Imperial Policy and South Africa.* Oxford: Clarendon Press, 1955.

Radcliffe-Brown, A. R., and Forde, Daryll (eds.). *African Systems of Kinship and Marriage*. London: Oxford University Press, 1950.

Raddatz, H. *The Transvaal and the Swaziland Gold Fields*. Cape Town: Saul Solomon, 1886.

Ramage, Sir Richard. *Report on the Structure of the Public Services in Basutoland, Bechuanaland, and Swaziland, 1961*. Cape Town: High Commissioner's Office, 1962.

Reeves, Ambrose. *Shooting at Sharpeville: The Agony of South Africa*. Boston: Houghton Mifflin, 1960; London: Gollancz, 1961.

————. *South Africa, Yesterday and Tomorrow*. London: Gollancz, 1962.

Regan, William Frederic. *Boer and Uitlander*. London: Digby, Long, 1896.

Rhoodie, Eschel. *The Third Africa*. New York: Twin Circle, 1968.

Ridpath, J. C., and Ellis, E. S. *The Story of South Africa*. Chicago: John Moore, 1899.

Roux, Edward. *Time Longer than Rope*. Madison: University of Wisconsin Press, 1964.

Sachs, B. *The Road from Sharpeville*. London: D. Dobson, 1961.

Sachs, E. S. *The Choice Before South Africa*. New York: Philosophical Library, 1952.

Sampson, A. *The Treason Cage*. London: Heinemann, 1958.

Schapera, Isaac. *Government and Politics in Tribal Societies*. London: Watts, 1956.

————. *The Bantu Speaking Tribes of South Africa*. London: Routledge, 1937.

————. *The Ethnic Composition of the Tswana Tribes*. London: London School of Economics, 1952.

————. *A Handbook of Tswana Law and Custom*. London and New York: Oxford University Press, 1938.

————. *Native Land Tenure in the Bechuanaland Protectorate*. Alice, South Africa: Lovedale Press, 1943.

————. *Migrant Labour and Tribal Life*. London and New York: Oxford University Press, 1947.

————. *Tribal Legislation Among the Tswana of the Bechuanaland Protectorate*. London: Lund, Humphries, 1943.

Scott, M. *A Time to Speak*. Garden City, N.Y.: Doubleday, 1958.

Scutt, Joan. *African Hands*. London: Edinburgh House Press, 1961.

————. *The Drums Are Beating*. London: South African General Mission, 1954.

Selwyn, James. *South of the Congo*. New York: Random House, 1943.

Silburn, P. A. B. *South Africa: White and Black—Brown?* London: Allen and Unwin, 1927.

Sillery, A. *The Bechuanaland Protectorate*. London and New York: Oxford University Press, 1952.

Sobhuza II, King. "Petition of King Sobhuza II to the British Government Concerning Mineral Rights." Mimeographed, Lobamba, 1941.

South Africa, Government of. *Negotiations Regarding the Transfer to the Union of South Africa of the Government of Basutoland, the Bechuanaland Protectorate, and Swaziland, 1910–1939.* Pretoria: Government Printer, 1953.

———. *Official Yearbook of the Union and of Basutoland, Bechuanaland Protectorate, and Swaziland.* Pretoria: Office of Census and Statistics, 1919–1934.

———. *High Commission Territories and the Union of South Africa.* London: Royal Institute of International Affairs, 1956.

———. *Debates of the House of Assembly, Vol. 106–115 (Hansard).* Cape Town: Cape Times, 1961, 1962, 1963, 1964, 1965.

Sowden, L. *The South African Union.* London: Hale, 1944.

Spence, J. E. *Lesotho: The Politics of Dependence.* London: Oxford University Press, 1968.

———. *Republic Under Pressure: A Study of South African Foreign Policy.* London: Oxford University Press, 1965.

Spooner, F. P. *South African Predicament.* New York: Praeger, 1961.

Stevens, R. P. *Lesotho, Botswana, and Swaziland: The Former High Commission Territories in Southern Africa.* New York: Praeger, 1967.

Swaziland Democratic Party. *Totalitarianism Opposed.* Mbabane: High Commission Printing and Publishing Company, 1962.

———. "Minutes." Mimeographed, n.p., 1962, 1963, 1964.

Swaziland Progressive Association. "Constitution of the Swaziland Progressive Association." Mimeographed, Mbabane, 1929.

Swaziland, Government of. *Annual Report of the Agricultural Department.* Mbabane: Government Printer, 1946, 1947, 1948, 1950, 1951, 1952, 1953, 1954, 1955, 1956, 1957, 1958, 1959, 1960, 1961, 1962, 1963.

———. *Annual Report of the Colonial Development and Welfare Schemes: Estimates of Revenues and Expenditures.* Mbabane: Government Printer, 1957, 1958, 1959, 1960, 1961, 1962, 1963, 1964, 1965, 1966.

———. *Annual Report of Commissioner of Police.* Mbabane: Government Printer, 1954, 1955, 1956, 1957, 1958, 1959, 1960, 1961, 1962, 1963, 1964.

———. *Annual Report of the Department of Education.* Mbabane: Government Printer, 1946, 1947, 1948, 1949, 1950, 1951, 1952, 1953.

———. *Annual Report of the Director of Public Works.* Mbabane: Government Printer, 1956, 1957, 1958, 1959, 1960, 1961, 1962, 1963, 1964.

———. *Annual Report Estimates of Revenue and Expenditure for the Financial Year, 1 April–31 March.* Mbabane: Government Printer, 1947, 1948, 1949, 1950, 1951, 1952, 1953, 1954, 1955, 1956, 1957, 1958, 1959, 1960, 1961, 1962, 1963, 1964, 1965, 1966.

————. *Annual Report of the Geological Survey.* Mbabane: Government Printer, 1950, 1951, 1952, 1953, 1954, 1955, 1956, 1957, 1958, 1959, 1960, 1961, 1962.

————. *Annual Report of the Land Utilization Department.* Mbabane: Government Printer, 1955, 1956, 1957, 1960, 1961, 1962, 1963, 1964.

————. *Annual Report of Medical and Sanitary Reports.* Mbabane: Government Printer, 1943, 1944, 1945, 1946, 1947, 1948, 1949, 1950, 1951, 1952, 1953, 1954, 1955, 1956, 1957, 1958, 1959, 1960, 1961, 1962, 1963, 1964.

————. *Annual Report of Natural Resources Board.* Mbabane: Government Printer, 1964.

————. *Annual Report of the Native Land Settlement Department.* Mbabane: Government Printer, 1956, 1957.

————. *Census of Swaziland, 1956.* Mbabane: Government Printer, 1958.

————. *Customs Union Agreement Between the Governments of Swaziland, Botswana, Lesotho, and South Africa.* Mbabane: Swaziland Government Gazette, 1969.

————. *The Five-Year Development Plan Covering the Period 1 April 1955 to 31 March 1960.* Mbabane: Government Printer, 1954.

————. "Joint Memorandum by the Leaders of the Elected Governments of Basutoland, Bechuanaland Protectorate, and Swaziland to the Heads of African States." Mimeographed, Accra, October 25, 1965.

————. *Official Gazette Proclamations.* Mbabane: Government Printer, 1951, 1952, 1953, 1954, 1955, 1956, 1957, 1958, 1959, 1960, 1961, 1962, 1963, 1964.

————. *Proposals for a Swaziland Constitution.* Mbabane: Government Printer, 1962.

————. "Public Statement on the Constitutional Conference." Mimeographed, London, February 14, 1936.

————. *Rules and Regulations of the High Court of Swaziland.* Cape Town: Richards, 1890.

————. *Swaziland Legislative Council Official Reports (Hansard).* Cape Town: Cape Times, 1964, 1965, 1966, 1967, 1968.

————. *What Is a Trade Union?* Mbabane: Government Printer, 1964.

————. European Advisory Council. "Minutes of the Reconstituted European Advisory Council." Mimeographed by the Government Secretary, Mbabane, 1947–1950, 1950–1953, 1954–1955, 1956, 1957, 1958, 1959, 1960, 1961, 1962, 1963, 1964.

Theal, George McCall. *The Portuguese in South Africa.* London: Fisher and Unwin, 1896.

Thompson, Leonard Monteath. *The Unification of South Africa*. Oxford: Clarendon Press, 1960.

Thompson, W. Scott. *Ghana's Foreign Policy, 1957–1966*. Princeton: Princeton University Press, 1969.

Tingston, H. S. G. *The Problem of South Africa*. London: Gollancz, 1955.

United Nations Agricultural and Rural Development Survey. *Selected Agricultural Statistics*. Mbabane: Government Printer, 1966.

United States House of Representatives Committee on Foreign Affairs. *South Africa and United States Foreign Policy*. Hearings April 2, 15, 1969. Washington: U.S. Government Printing Office, 1969.

Van den Berghe, P. L. *Caneville: The Social Structure of a South African Town*. Middletown: Wesleyan University Press, 1964.

Vandenbosch, Amry. *South Africa and the World: The Foreign Policy of Apartheid*. Lexington: University Press of Kentucky, 1970.

Van Rensburg, P. *Guilty Land: The History of Apartheid*. New York: Praeger, 1962.

Vansina, Jan. *Kingdoms of the Savanna*. Madison: University of Wisconsin Press, 1966.

van Velsen, Jan. *The Politics of Kinship*. Manchester: Manchester University Press, 1967.

van Wyk, A. J. *Swaziland: A Political Study*. Pretoria: Africa Institute of South Africa, 1969.

———. *Lesotho: A Political Survey*. Pretoria: Africa Institute of South Africa, 1967.

Vatcher, W. H. *White Laager: The Rise of Afrikaner Nationalism*. New York: Praeger, 1965.

Verwoerd, Hendrick. *The Road to Freedom for Basutoland, Bechuanaland, and Swaziland*. Pretoria: Government Printer, 1963.

Walker, E. A. *South Africa*. Oxford: Clarendon Press, 1940.

——— (ed.). *Cambridge History of the British Empire*. Vol. 8 (South Africa, Rhodesia, and the High Commission Territories). Cambridge: Cambridge University Press, 1963.

Walker, Eric. *A History of Southern Africa*. London: Longmans, Green, 1957.

Watts, C. C. *Dawn in Swaziland*. London: Society for the Propagation of the Gospel in Foreign Parts, 1922.

Way, H. J. R. *Mineral Ownership as Affecting Mineral Development of Swaziland*. Mbabane: Government Printer, 1955.

Webster, John, and Mohome, Paulus. *A Bibliography on Swaziland*. Syracuse: Maxwell School of Citizenship and Public Affairs, 1968.

Whitaker, C. S. *The Politics of Tradition: Continuity and Change in Northern Nigeria*. Princeton: Princeton University Press, 1970.

Williams, Hugh (ed.). *Selected Official Documents of the South*

African Republic and Great Britain. Philadelphia: American Academy of Political and Social Science, 1900.

Williams, J. G. *Moshesh: The Man on the Mountain.* London: Oxford University Press, 1950.

Wilson, Monica, and Thompson, Leonard (eds.). *The Oxford History of South Africa.* Vol. 1. London: Oxford University Press, 1969.

Wilson, William. *England and the Transvaal.* London: Grosvenor Press, 1899.

Worsfold, William Basil. *The Reconstruction of the New Colonies Under Lord Milner.* London: Trench, Tuger, 1913.

———. *The Union of South Africa.* Boston: Little, Brown Press, 1913.

Ziervogel, Dirk. *A Grammar of Swazi.* Johannesburg: University of Witwatersrand Press, 1952.

———. *Swazi Texts.* Pretoria: van Schaik, 1957.

Index

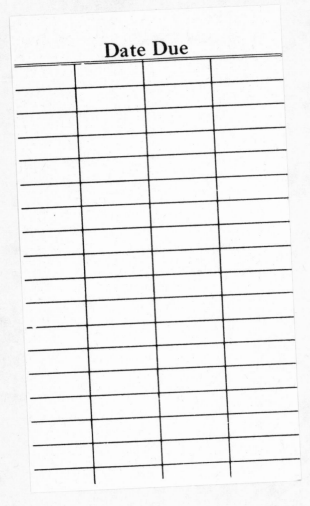

Date Due